Proverbs

Selected Books in the
SkyLight Illuminations Series

Proverbs

Annotated & Explained

Translation & annotation by Rabbi Rami Shapiro

For People of All Faiths, All Backgrounds

JEWISH LIGHTS Publishing

Nashville, Tennessee

Walking Together, Finding the Way ®

SKYLIGHT PATHS®
PUBLISHING

Nashville, Tennessee

Proverbs: Annotated & Explained

Translation, annotation, and introductory material © 2011 by Rami Shapiro

Library of Congress Cataloging-in-Publication Data
Bible. O.T. Proverbs. English. Shapiro. 2011.
Proverbs : annotated & explained / translation & annotation by Rami Shapiro.
    p. cm. — (Skylight illuminations series)
Includes bibliographical references.
ISBN 978-1-59473-310-9 (pbk.) — ISBN 978-1-68336-245-6 (hc)
1. Bible. O.T. Proverbs—Criticism, interpretation, etc. I. Shapiro, Rami M. II. Title.
BS1463.S525 2011
223'.706—dc23

2011025877

10   9   8   7   6   5   4   3   2

Manufactured in the United States of America

SkyLight Paths Publishing is creating a place where people of different spiritual traditions come together for challenge and inspiration, a place where we can help each other understand the mystery that lies at the heart of our existence.

SkyLight Paths sees both believers and seekers as a community that increasingly transcends traditional boundaries of religion and denomination—people wanting to learn from each other, *walking together, finding the way.*

SkyLight Paths, "Walking Together, Finding the Way" and colophon are trademarks of LongHill Partners, Inc., registered in the U.S. Patent and Trademark Office.

Published by SkyLight Paths Publishing/Jewish Lights Publishing
An imprint of Turner Publishing Company
4507 Charlotte Avenue, Suite 100
Nashville, Tennessee 37209
Tel: (615) 255-2665
www.skylightpaths.com   www.jewishlights.com

Contents ☐

Preface ☐

The world of the biblical Book of Proverbs, *Sefer Mishlei*, is fairly black-and-white. King Solomon, the presumed author of the book, eliminates the grays of life, an elimination I at first found troubling. The more I sought to apply these teachings to my own life, however, the more I realized that much of what I took for legitimate gray was in fact my own attempt to blur what was clearly black-and-white. I preferred to think in terms of gray to rationalize away questionable actions or to confuse things so that I could avoid doing the right thing.

The fact is, life is fairly simple. There is birth and death; good and evil; right and wrong; justice and injustice; honesty and dishonesty. We complicate life by refusing to respond to reality as it is. Most of the time it is not difficult to identify the right path. What is difficult is actually walking it.

Many years ago on a flight from Miami to Chicago, I struck up a conversation with the man sitting next me, a financial analyst named Jason. When I told him I was a rabbi, he paused for a long moment and said, "I'm dying. I have a rare form of cancer, and there is nothing anyone can do for me. I'm forty-six years old. I have a wife and three kids. The oldest is only nine. How the hell does this happen to people? And why the hell is it happening to me?

"My closest friend says I have to experience this cancer in order to work out some error in a past life. My priest says it's God's will. What kind of God wills this?"

Jason seemed a bit out of breath. I invited him to keep talking, but he had nothing more to say. It was my turn.

"Listen, Jason, I can't pretend to know what you're going through. I have no solution to offer, nor any way to make sense of your cancer.

I can give you my opinion on some of the issues you raised, but that's about it."

Jason nodded, and I continued.

"There is no reason why this is happening to you. And saying this is God's will is simply another way of saying horrible things happen. They do, and you are living proof. I believe in reality, and the reality is that you are a young man with a wife and three young children, and you are dying. Asking 'Why me?' is a distraction from that reality. There is no final answer to 'Why me?' You can invent possibilities right up until the moment you die, and none of them will really satisfy you.

"Jason, I'm not trying to be harsh, just clear. You are going to hear a lot of opinions about why this is happening to you. Most of it is offered in order to comfort the person offering it. The only comfort you can find in your situation is to respond to it with the best that is in you."

"What does that mean?" Jason asked.

"You have to do what you can to maintain your health for as long as possible. You have to do what you can to see to the financial security of your family. And you have to do what you can to show your kids the right way to die."

"The right way to die?"

"Show them that death is sad, maybe even tragic, and that people can handle the sad and the tragic in a loving way. Love them so much that you are willing to share your feelings with them. Love them so much that you are willing to spend as much time with them as they need. Love them so much that you do not close the door of your heart to them when you are the most lost and they are the most frightened."

"The only thing I'm sure of is that I'm dying and that I love my wife and kids," Jason said.

"That's reality," I said. "Now respond to it."

"Just die and love?"

"The other way around," I said. "Just love and die."

When I share this story with people, they often criticize me for being unduly harsh and cold. You may feel the same way. The fact is that I had only a few minutes to get to the heart of a very serious matter. I could have complicated things sufficiently to pass the time on the airplane and leave Jason with a lot of theoretical ideas to ponder. But that would have been a cop-out. Life isn't that complicated. His situation was extremely simple: love and die. Maybe the same could be said of all of us.

The Book of Proverbs addresses us as if we were all Jasons in need of clarity and truth. No theories. No excuses. Just love and die. It is this ability of Proverbs to cut to the heart of the matter that gives the book its power. It doesn't deal in grays.

For Solomon, there are two states of mind: disciplined and slothful. The disciplined mind focuses on the task at hand and engages life as best it can. The slothful mind looks for excuses for inaction or seeks to cut corners through violence, dishonesty, and theft.

Solomon calls us "ignorant," "lazy," and "foolish" when we complicate the simple and substitute the easy for the good. He calls us "wise" when we cease to hide from reality and openly and honestly face the truth of each moment.

Is Solomon wrong to approach life so simply? Are his proverbs any less useful for their being so stark? On the contrary, it is Solomon's honest portrayal of reality and his clear prescriptions for how to live it that give the book its power and timelessness.

To benefit from reading Solomon's proverbs, you have to have the courage to see the world as he does: simply, and without the smoke and mirrors of our rationalizations and excuses. The Book of Proverbs forces us to examine our lives and how we are living them without the benefit of psychological sophistry and New Age babble. We are either disciplined or lazy. We are either doing good or doing bad. We are either curbing our desires or succumbing to them. We are either wise or foolish. We are either a student of wisdom or a puppet of desire.

Facing this is a challenge. Your mind will find excuses to discount almost every teaching. You need to be patient with yourself, but not yielding. Solomon's teachings are simple, but not simplistic. If you allow them to speak to you honestly, if you do not defend yourself against their meaning and their implication for your life, and if you listen carefully to this ancient king's instructions, you will change for the better and grow in wisdom.

Introduction □

Why do you read the Bible? I ask this question of people all across the United States as part of various seminars I teach. When I ask this question of Jews, I most often get a variation on this response provided by a forty-something Sunday school teacher at a Reform temple in Florida: "The *TaNaCH* [the Hebrew Bible] is the history book of my people, and I read it to find out where I came from, and what it means to be a Jew, one of God's chosen people."

A twenty-year-old fundamentalist Protestant taking my class on the Bible at Middle Tennessee State University told me, "I don't just read the Bible for this class. I read it for myself, my soul, and my salvation. I read it because God wrote it, and if I pay attention to what I read and what He said, I will know what He wants me to believe about God and man and salvation, and that will get me right with God and into heaven."

These are both good answers, but not ones that satisfy me personally. I don't believe the Bible is history, at least not history in the way we think of history today. If I read a book on the history of the Revolutionary War or on the history of civil rights legislation in the United States, I expect to read facts. Of course, authors are going to interpret those historical facts—verifiable events—and different historians will interpret facts in different ways, but it never occurs to me that the authors are making up the history they are reporting.

Modern historians have to verify the facts they report and interpret. Biblical historians were not similarly constrained. They were writing what we might call historical fiction: the events they recorded may or may not have happened, but the message is in the story rather than the history.

We can argue about the historical accuracy of the Bible all we want, but for those of us interested in the Book of Proverbs, the point is moot. Unlike most of the Bible, which purports to be historically accurate, the Book of Proverbs is story-free. The teachings it proclaims are independent of the times in which they were first composed. So no one reads the Book of Proverbs for history.

And no one reads it to find out what God commands, because God doesn't command anything at all in the Book of Proverbs. The book, while talking a bit about God, is essentially secular. It is concerned with wisdom, practical truths about how to live wisely and well. The truth of the proverbs found in the Book of Proverbs isn't backed up with "Thus saith the Lord." These proverbs are true (or false) because, upon observation, you and I see them to be true (or false). Unlike almost anything else in the Bible, the truths claimed in the Book of Proverbs are testable and verifiable. This alone makes the Book of Proverbs worth reading.

The Nature of Hebrew Proverbs
Every culture has its proverbial sayings. More often than not they are fairly prosaic observations of life upon which a person can build a workable philosophy for living. In the mid-eighteenth century, for example, from 1734 to 1747, Ben Franklin wrote more than six hundred proverbs and published them in his *Poor Richard's Almanack*. Here is just a sampling:

"Necessity never made a good bargain" (1735)
"God helps them that help themselves" (1736)
"Industry, Perseverance, & Frugality, make Fortune yield" (1744)

These simple sayings are guides to right living, demanding nothing more from you than memory and application. The Hebrew Bible also contains this kind of proverb, but the Book of Proverbs itself is much more than a Jewish predecessor to *Poor Richard*.

Compare Franklin's proverb "A penny saved is a penny earned" with Proverbs 13:11, "Wealth hastily gotten will dwindle, but those who gather little by little will increase it" (NRSV). Close your eyes and repeat these two proverbs aloud. Chances are you remember Franklin's version, while the biblical text is muddled. Although both proverbs share a common message, Franklin's version is designed for memorizing, while the biblical text seems needlessly convoluted.

This isn't an accident. The proverbs found in the Book of Proverbs are more than commonplace truisms. They are complex poetic forms designed to have an effect on the reader or listener beyond that of mere assent. The Book of Proverbs is an anthology of teachings—some dealing with ordinary events, some with dimensions far beyond the ordinary—designed not so much for the average Hebrew living in the seventh century BCE, but for the literati, that class of thinker belonging to the Hebrew wisdom school.

Wisdom literature exists in every culture, and biblical wisdom comes to the party quite late. By the time the Book of Proverbs was compiled sometime in the seventh century BCE, Egyptian wisdom texts already dated back more than thirteen hundred years earlier. Among the oldest of the Egyptian texts is the *Instruction of Amen-em-opet*, compiled sometime between the thirteenth and tenth centuries BCE. The thirty sayings of Amen-em-opet son of Kanakht were written down as instructions to his son or perhaps to his students (or both) and set forth the qualities a person needs to cultivate in order to enjoy a happy and productive life: humility, self-control, generosity, truthfulness, and modesty.

Such books of instruction often take the form of a father's advice to his son. Indeed, this is how the Bible's Book of Proverbs defines itself: "Hear, my child, your father's instruction, and do not reject your mother's teaching" (Proverbs 1:8, NRSV). While it may have been true in ancient Egypt that children were educated at home by their parents, by the time of *Instruction of Amen-em-opet* and certainly centuries later when the Book of Proverbs was composed, parents were replaced by wisdom sages, and the language of teaching was far more literary than oral.

Here is the opening text of *Instruction of Amen-em-opet*:

Beginning of the teaching for life,
The instructions for well-being,
Every rule for relations with elders,
For conduct toward magistrates;
Knowing how to answer one who speaks,
To reply to one who sends a message.
So as to direct him on the paths of life,
To make him prosper upon earth;
To let his heart enter its shrine,
Steering clear of evil;
To save him from the mouth of strangers,
To let [him] be praised in the mouth of people.
Made by the overseer of fields, experienced in his office.

(*INSTRUCTION OF AMEN-EM-OPET*, 1, 1–13)

Compare this with the opening of the Book of Proverbs:

These are the proverbs and parables of Solomon, son of David,
    king of Israel;
A guide to insight, understanding, and spiritual discipline
to help you become generous, honest, and balanced.
They are offered to the simple that they may gain knowledge;
to the young that they may find direction;
to the learned that they might peer behind the words and attain
    wisdom,
for I speak in riddles both simple and profound,
wise words that hide deeper meanings.

(PROVERBS 1:1–7)

The fact that the ancient Hebrew wisdom sages borrowed from and adapted far more ancient forms of expression should not be surprising. Egyptian wisdom literature represented the pinnacle of literary arts, and any educator seeking to instill wisdom in students would look to and borrow from the masters of the age. This is not to say that the wisdom teachings themselves are the same. Biblical wisdom literature reflects the experience and mindset of the Hebrew people and should not be read as merely derivative of ancient Egypt.

The authors of 1 Kings, written at the same time as the Book of Proverbs, make it clear that Jewish wisdom surpasses the older wisdom of Egypt:

> Solomon's wisdom surpassed the wisdom of all the people of the east, and all the wisdom of Egypt. He was wiser than anyone else, wiser than Ethan the Ezrahite, and Heman, Calcol, and Darda, children of Mahol; his fame spread throughout all the surrounding nations.
>
> (1 KINGS 4:30–31, NRSV)

Egypt is not the only influence on Hebrew wisdom literature. Sumerian, Babylonian, and Assyrian wisdom also seems to have provided the Hebrew sages with both models and content. Unlike their Egyptian counterparts, who provided wisdom in the form of instructions, Mesopotamian wisdom often focused on articulating basic truisms about life. For example, the *Words of Ahikar*, an Assyrian text written around the same time as the Book of Proverbs, tells us:

> The son who is educated and disciplined and whose feet are fettered will do well. Do not hesitate to take the rod to your son if you cannot restrain him from wickedness. If I strike you, my son, you will not die, and if I leave you to your own devices you will not live.
>
> (LINES 80–82, IN WHYBRAY, *WISDOM IN PROVERBS*, P. 6)

Its Hebrew parallel reads:

> Do not withhold discipline from your children; if you beat them with a rod, they will not die. If you beat them with the rod, you will save their lives from Sheol.
>
> (PROVERBS 23:13–14, NRSV)

The similarity between wisdom literatures suggests that the sages of different cultures shared insights with one another, often providing their colleagues with prompts for their own writings. Yet this doesn't mean that Hebrew wisdom literature merely mirrors that of the surrounding cultures of Egypt and Mesopotamia. On the contrary, there are some features unique to the Book of Proverbs.

First, the sages of Israel spoke to a broader audience than the scholars of Egypt. While some of the proverbs contained in the Book of Proverbs reflect the instructional manuals of Egypt, others speak to a more general audience, suggesting that literacy among the Hebrews of the seventh century BCE was more widespread than it was in neighboring Egypt.

Second, while all wisdom literature urges the reader to adhere to the divine order of life, only the Book of Proverbs sees that order as the work of a single deity. The gods of Israel's neighbors were themselves under the influence of an impersonal force, while the God of Israel was seen as the ultimate force in the universe. In the Book of Proverbs, unlike non-Jewish wisdom literature, the source of wisdom is God, and adhering to the way of the wisdom brings you under the protection of God, "for the Lord gives wisdom and from his mouth comes knowledge and understanding" (Proverbs 2:6, NRSV). As we shall see, Wisdom is God's daughter, the first of God's creations, whereas in other cultures, wisdom is independent from gods and goddesses.

Linking wisdom with God did raise some eyebrows in ancient Israel. These books were not written in isolation. Along with the wisdom of the sages was the wisdom of the prophets, and their literatures often clashed. For example, in its guidance to the ruling class, Proverbs does not mention God: "For want of strategy an army falls, but victory comes with much planning" (Proverbs 11:14, JPS); in a similar passage in the book of the prophet Zechariah we read, "Not by might, nor by power, but by My spirit— said the Lord of Hosts" (Zechariah 4:6, JPS).

Another area of conflict between Hebrew wisdom literature and the rest of the Hebrew Bible is the focus of wisdom sages on universal human concerns rather than particular Jewish ones. Although it is clearly a Jewish book referencing Solomon, Hezekiah, and the God of Israel, the Book of Proverbs appears completely uninterested in Jewish history or destiny. Although God is still the master of the universe, Proverbs offers no hint that

God has a special relationship with the Jewish people or their Promised Land. Where chapter after chapter in the rest of the Bible deals with God's relationship with Israel, God's love for Israel, God's anger at Israel, God's jealousy vis-à-vis other gods and their relationship to Israel, the Book of Proverbs sees God as a universal power who transcends nationality and politics.

The lack of nationalism in the Book of Proverbs brings us to its corollary: its focus on the individual as an individual. Wisdom isn't for the nation as a whole, but for the individual person alone. True, if most people adhere to these teachings of wisdom, the nation will thrive, but this is neither stated nor is it of any concern. Proverbs is a book for the individual person.

It is this focus on the individual that makes the Book of Proverbs in particular, and Hebrew wisdom literature in general, so contemporary. Ours is an age of the individual. We speak of self-responsibility over group responsibility. We hold the individual accountable for what she does, and not the group from which she comes.

Who Wrote the Book of Proverbs?

As noted above, tradition ascribes authorship of Proverbs to King Solomon, who according to Jewish legend was the wisest human being not only of his time but of any time.

> At Gibeon the Lord appeared to Solomon in a dream by night; and God said, "Ask what I should give you." And Solomon said, "You have shown great and steadfast love to your servant my father David, because he walked before you in faithfulness, in righteousness, and in uprightness of heart toward you; and you have kept for him this great and steadfast love, and have given him a son to sit on his throne today. And now, O Lord my God, you have made your servant king in place of my father David, although I am only a little child; I do not know how to go out or come in. And your servant is in the midst of the people whom you have chosen, a great people, so numerous they cannot be numbered or counted. Give your servant therefore an understanding mind to govern your people, able to discern between good and evil; for who can govern this your great people?"

It pleased the Lord that Solomon had asked this. God said to him, "Because you have asked this, and have not asked for yourself long life or riches, or for the life of your enemies, but have asked for yourself understanding to discern what is right, I now do according to your word. Indeed I give you a wise and discerning mind; no one like you has been before you and no one like you shall arise after you. I give you also what you have not asked, both riches and honor all your life; no other king shall compare with you. If you will walk in my ways, keeping my statutes and my commandments, as your father David walked, then I will lengthen your life."

Then Solomon awoke; it had been a dream. He came to Jerusalem where he stood before the ark of the covenant of the Lord. He offered up burnt offerings and offerings of well-being, and provided a feast for all his servants.

(1 KINGS 3:5–13, NRSV)

Most us were taught that Solomon lived in the tenth century BCE, was the son of King David, and reigned as king over an undivided Israel, a vast expanse of land stretching from Syria to the Red Sea, with Jerusalem as its capital. In addition to the literary works ascribed to him by Jewish tradition—the Book of Proverbs, Ecclesiastes, and Song of Songs—Solomon was most famous for the glorious Temple he built to the God of Israel. The truth, however, is somewhat less imposing.

Solomon was David's son and did reign from Jerusalem over a united Israel, but the country he ruled was anything but vast, and the city from which he governed was anything but lavish and literate. Even the Temple of Solomon may not have existed in Solomon's day, with the earliest archeological evidence dating from the eighth century BCE rather than the tenth in which Solomon lived.

What we know of Solomon from the Bible was written centuries after his reign, during the time of King Josiah at the closing of the seventh century BCE. His legend reflects the hopes and dreams of Josiah's time rather than the facts of Solomon's time.

I would not go so far as to doubt the existence of King Solomon or his father, David, but it is not too much to say that most of what we know about him is surely exaggerated. For example, the Bible tells us that Solomon "made silver as common in Jerusalem as stones" (1 Kings 10:27), when archeological evidence suggests that Solomon's Jerusalem was not much more than a minor hamlet. And the fact shared in 1 Kings 11:3 that he was wed to seven hundred princesses, and had three hundred concubines on the side, seems a bit overblown even by ancient royal standards of political marriage. And, for all his wisdom, wealth, and sexual prowess, there is no mention of Solomon in any Egyptian or Mesopotamian text dating to his time. Even archeological evidence of his famed Temple is lacking.

This is not to say that David and Solomon are literary creations of seventh-century-BCE writers of historical fiction. On the contrary, in 1993 a fragment of a monument was found at Tel Dan in northern Israel proclaiming in Aramaic the 835 BCE victory of Hazael, king of Damascus, over the army of the Northern Kingdom of Israel:

> [I killed Jeho]ram son of [Ahab] king of Israel, and [I] killed [Ahaz]iahu son of [Jehoram kin]g of the House of David. And I set [their towns into ruins and turned] their land into [desolation].

This fragment proves the existence of the Davidic line. A similar fragment found in the nineteenth century by the shores of the Dead Sea, inscribed by the ninth-century-BCE Moabite king Mesha, also mentions the House of David, leaving no doubt that the Davidic dynasty was known throughout the region. What is in doubt is the power and reach of the kingdom David founded and that Solomon, so we are told, expanded.

The region of Judah in which Jerusalem sits was not conducive to empire building. The land was largely parched desert, sparsely populated, and incapable of sustaining large armies. Jerusalem in Solomon's day was more a village than a great urban center, and as was mentioned earlier, there is no archeological evidence that Solomon had the wealth or manpower to take and hold an empire.

Arguments to the contrary, however, are not hard to find; they are just hard to swallow. The famous Israeli archeologist Yigal Yadin, for example, wrote of his ascribing the city of Hazor to Solomon:

> There is no example in the history of archeology where a passage helped so much in identifying and dating structures in several of the most important tells in the Holy Land as has I Kings 9:15.... Our decision to attribute that layer [at Hazor] to Solomon was based primarily on the I Kings passage, the stratigraphy, and the pottery. But when in addition we found in that stratum a six-chambered, two-towered gate connected to a casemate wall identical in plan and measurement with the gate at Megiddo, we felt sure we had successfully identified Solomon's city. (Yadin, in *Bible Unearthed*, by Israel Finkelstein [New York: The Free Press, 2001], p. 140)

The problem is that subsequent review of these finds proves much less convincing. The style of pottery and architecture that so impressed Dr. Yadin are now known to date to the ninth rather than the tenth century BCE, making them irrelevant to Solomon, who had died decades earlier. Carbon-14 dating techniques unavailable to Dr. Yadin confirm that his conclusions were wrong. And so is the Bible.

Written in the seventh century BCE, hundreds of years after the death of Solomon, the legends of this all-wise king took on the patina of history. Biblical authors writing during the height of Judah's power, when Jerusalem was indeed a great urban center and the Temple was a central point of worship, imagined an even greater time in the not-so-distant past when the Davidic kingdom was unified and stretched from Syria in the north to the Red Sea in the south. Judah's armies and government in the seventh century BCE were superior to her neighbors, and so her historians imagined they had always been so.

So while Solomon's name is referenced in Proverbs 1:1, "The proverbs and parables of Solomon, son of David, king of Israel," chances are Solomon himself is not the author of Proverbs. Other authors are mentioned in the text itself—Agur and Lemuel (Proverbs 30:1 and Proverbs

31:1, respectively)—though these names came to be considered nick-names for Solomon and don't even appear in the Septuagint, the Greek translation of the Hebrew Bible written by Jewish scholars in Alexandria during the third and second centuries BCE. Most likely the Book of Proverbs was written some two hundred plus years after the death of Solomon, by a variety of authors who, seeking to impose a unity and gravitas on their work, chose Solomon as their pseudonym.

One Book, Seven Collections of Sayings

Knowing that the Book of Proverbs is the product of multiple authors, we can actually discern seven different collections of sayings that were blended into a single book:

Book One: The Nine Foundational Teachings (Proverbs 1:1–9:18)
Book Two: The First Collection of Shorter Sayings (Proverbs 10:1–22:16)
Book Three: The Thirty Precepts of Wisdom (Proverbs 22:17–24:22)
Book Four: Sayings of Solomon's Contemporaries (Proverbs 24:23–34)
Book Five: The Second Collection of Shorter Sayings (Proverbs 25–29)
Book Six: Warnings and Numerical Proverbs (Proverbs 30:1–33)
Book Seven: A Mother's Advice (Proverbs 31:1–31)

Some scholars break this final book into two by separating "A Woman of Valor" (Proverbs 31:10–31) from the rest. All of these writings probably date to the seventh century BCE, though they may contain sayings that are much older. Here is a brief summary of the seven books of Proverbs:

BOOK ONE: THE NINE FOUNDATIONAL TEACHINGS

This collection sets out the intention of the Book of Proverbs to function as a guide to wisdom and spiritual discipline.

From the beginning, the authors tell us that they speak in riddles, dark sayings, teachings that must be unpacked rather than simply memorized. This is one of the things that sets the Book of Proverbs apart from similar wisdom sayings from surrounding cultures such as Egypt and Mesopotamia. The Book of Proverbs is a kind of code, closer to the koans of the Zen Buddhist tradition than the proverbs of *Poor Richard*. I will do my best to decode the dark sayings in the commentary that accompanies this translation.

The most mysterious material in book 1 deals with Chochmah (literally, "Wisdom"), the firstborn daughter of God who is the means of creation and the way of its preservation. We will speak at length about her later in this introduction.

BOOK TWO: THE FIRST COLLECTION OF SHORTER SAYINGS

The thirteen chapters that comprise book 2 are essentially simple sayings relating to practical matters that need little explanation. Here are some representative samples:

Death cannot be bribed,
but generosity outlasts the grave.

(PROVERBS 10:2)

In famine wisdom fills the belly;
while sin brings starvation even in the midst of plenty.

(PROVERBS 10:3)

Tip the balance by lying and your life is impoverished;
uphold honesty and the result is prosperity.

(PROVERBS 10:4)

The wise learn from the softest whisper;
the ignorant sleep through the loudest alarm.

(PROVERBS 10:5)

BOOK THREE: THE THIRTY PRECEPTS OF WISDOM

The proverbs in this third collection of teachings bear striking resemblance to the far older Egyptian collection of sayings called the *Instruction of Amen-em-opet*, discussed earlier. In it, Amen-em-opet makes a distinction between the "silent ones," who go about their business quietly, and the "heated ones," who are forever causing discord. Proverbs makes a similar distinction between the wise and the foolish. Amen-em-opet also speaks of Maat, the Egyptian goddess of order, both personal and cosmic, who may find her place in the Bible as Chochmah in the Book of Proverbs.

The text of the *Instruction of Amen-em-opet* helps us understand what was long thought to be a scribal error in Proverbs 22:20. The Hebrew text contains a word that is unintelligible: *shelshom*. In 1924, the noted Egyptologist Adolf Erman sought help in understanding this typo by comparing Proverbs 22:20 with *Amen-em-opet*, chapter 30, line 539:

> Here I will give you in writing *shelshom* principles of knowledge
>   that you need.
>
> (PROVERBS 22:20)

> Look to these thirty chapters; they inform, they educate.
>
> (*AMEN-EM-OPET*, CHAPTER 30, LINE 539)

In light of *Amen-em-opet, shelshom* should be read as *sheloshim*, "thirty." Here are some additional parallels between the third book of Proverbs and *Instruction of Amen-em-opet*:

> Do not exploit the defenseless, nor take advantage of the poor.
>
> (PROVERBS 22:22)

> Guard yourself against robbing the oppressed and against
>   overhearing the disabled.
>
> (*AMEN-EM-OPET*, P. 420A)

> Do not entertain anger, or be tempted by rage.
>
> (PROVERBS 22:24)

> Do not associate with a heated man, nor engage him in conversation.
>
> (*AMEN-EM-OPET*, P. 423A)

Be wary when dining with the powerful.

(PROVERBS 23:1A)

Do not eat bread before a noble.

(AMEN-EM-OPET, P. 424A)

Do not berate yourself for having less.

(PROVERBS 23:4A)

Cast not your heart in pursuit of riches.

(AMEN-EM-OPET, P. 422B)

BOOK FOUR: SAYINGS OF SOLOMON'S CONTEMPORARIES

This short collection of only twelve verses offers fairly commonsense advice regarding honoring your neighbor and diligence in your own labor.

BOOK FIVE: THE SECOND COLLECTION OF SHORTER SAYINGS

While overtly credited to King Solomon, this collection of sayings is said to have been written down by the "men of Hezekiah" (Proverbs 25:1). The implication here may be that these sayings attributed to Solomon may have been the foundational principles by which Hezekiah ruled. Unlike previous sayings in the Book of Proverbs, those found in book five tend to focus on the doings of kings and princes, what I have chosen to render here as "wise leaders."

BOOK SIX: WARNINGS AND NUMERICAL PROVERBS

This single chapter contains the proverbs of Agur, son of Jakeh. The opening line in Hebrew tells us that Agur was *hamassa*, which many scholars take to mean that Agur was a Massaite, a man from the land of Mash located between Judea and Babylonia. An alternative view put forth by the nineteenth-century Jewish historian Heinrich Graetz holds that *hamassa* is a corrupted version of *hamoshel*, a compiler of proverbs. Graetz's position seems simpler and more compelling.

Rabbinic commentary on Proverbs 30 insists that Agur was another name for Solomon. The Rabbis base their position on an interesting reading of the Hebrew. *Agur*, they say, means "one who compiles proverbs." *Jakeh* (*y-k-h*), they argue, is derived from the Hebrew *y-r-k*, "to spit." Solomon was one who compiled proverbs and spit on the word of God by marrying wives who were not followers of the Jewish God and who led him to worship other gods beside the God of Israel (Babylonian Talmud, *Berachot* 55a).

The proverbs attributed to Agur deal with skepticism, doubt, and faith.

BOOK SEVEN: A MOTHER'S ADVICE

Following the sayings of Agur come the proverbs of Lemuel. The name Lemuel was taken by the Rabbis to mean "one who belongs to" (*lemu*) "God" (*el*), and they saw the name as another reference to Solomon. There is no other reference to any Lemuel in the Bible, though this alone doesn't substantiate the claim that Lemuel was Solomon. He could just as easily be another sage devoted to God. Whoever Lemuel was, these are not his sayings, but those of his mother. The first part of the collection is her advice against the dangers of alcohol. The second, called "A Woman of Valor," is her description of the kind of woman she wants her daughters to be and her son to marry.

Proverb Styles

The writers of the Hebrew proverbs wrote in a number of literary styles but favored seven in particular. The first form is that of "*x* equals *y*," where the first phrase equals or necessitates the second: "Deceive someone by flattery and you will be deceived in the same manner" (Proverbs 29:5). The second pattern is just the opposite: "*x* does not equal *y*," for example, "A tranquil mind curbs desire, a disturbed mind mistakes even the bitter for the sweet" (Proverbs 27:7). The third pattern is "*x* is like *y*": "Like a thin cloak in winter, or wine mixed with vinegar, is a song of joy to a saddened heart" (Proverbs 25:20). The fourth style focuses on mockery: "As a door turns on its hinge, so the lazy turn on their beds" (Proverbs 26:14). The fifth type rests on classification: "The wise child welcomes the advice of elders; the foolish ignores anything they suggest" (Proverbs 13:1). The sixth form relies on relative values: "the more of *x* the more of *y*; the less of *x*, the less of *y*," for example, "Your good name is your greatest treasure; your reputation more precious than silver or gold" (Proverbs 22:1). The seventh form speaks to human nature and behavior: "Happiness illumines the face in joy, but a sad heart shrouds the spirit in despair" (Proverbs 15:13).

The Spiritual Message of Proverbs

Given the fact that the Book of Proverbs is a compilation of sayings or a collection of different books of sayings, it may be a stretch to say there is one spiritual message to be found here. Yet, to pretend there isn't some unifying theme regarding spiritual matters goes too far in the other direction.

At the heart of the Book of Proverbs is the figure of Chochmah, "Wisdom." She is the first of God's creations, and the blueprint by which all creation is formed. Wisdom is the way the world is the world. She may be compared to the current of an ocean or the grain of jade or wood. And as with wood, to work with Wisdom (as opposed to working against her) is to live an effective and satisfactory life. How do we live with wisdom?

The answer to this question is suggested in Proverbs 9:10, "*Yirat HaShem* is the beginning of wisdom." The phrase *yirat HaShem* is commonly, albeit misleadingly, rendered into English as "fear of the Lord." First, *yirat* can mean both "fear" and "awe," and either would be a legitimate translation of the Hebrew. Choosing "fear" over "awe" gives the phrase *yirat HaShem* an emotional quality of alarm that "awe" clearly lacks, and which the authors of these sayings may not intend.

Second, translating *HaShem* as "Lord" assigns gender to God and places "him" at the head of a hierarchical system reflective of the patriarchal hierarchy operative in ancient times. Such a rendering, however, is completely independent of the actual Hebrew of the text.

The Hebrew, rendered here as *HaShem*, literally "the Name," is the four-letter ineffable name of God: *Yod-Heh-Vav-Heh*. Because of the prohibition against pronouncing the name of God, sometime in the third century BCE, the euphemism *Adonai*, "Lord," became the accepted stand-in for the unpronounceable four-letter Name of God. So, *yirat HaShem* is not "fear of the Lord" but "fear of *Yod-Heh-Vav-Heh*."

Yod-Heh-Vav-Heh is the singular, future imperfect form of the Hebrew verb "to be," reflecting the self-revelation of God to Moses at the Burning Bush, *Ehyeh asher Ehyeh*, "I will be what I will be" (Exodus 3:14). Hebrew lacks a present tense for the verb "to be," and thus the more common translation of *Ehyeh asher Ehyeh* as "I am that I am" locks the biblical notion of God into a static mode that the Hebrew does not allow. The Hebrew God is not a noun but a verb; not a being or even the Supreme Being, but *be-ing* itself.

If we were to conjure a modern euphemism for *Yod-Heh-Vav-Heh* and *Ehyeh asher Ehyeh*, we might be better served with "that which is happening," or Be-ing, where be-ing implies the ongoing creative process of life, death, and new life rather than a static source outside the process. With this understanding of *yirat HaShem*, we might more accurately read our proverb to say, "Awe of reality is the beginning of knowledge, wisdom, and character disdained by fools." Standing in awe of reality is quite different from standing in fear of the Lord.

The question now becomes, what is the correlation between *Yod-Heh-Vav-Heh* and Chochmah, "Wisdom"? Let me suggest that Chochmah is the personification of *HaShem*. While God is clearly anthropomorphized in the Hebrew Bible, there is no corresponding understanding of God in the Book of Proverbs. God as *Yod-Heh-Vav-Heh* is the abstract reality of which we are comprised and in which we function. *Yod-Heh-Vav-Heh* is far closer to St. Paul's notion of God as that "in whom we live and move and have our being" (Acts 17:28) than to the all-too-human God of the Hebrew Bible. Yet it is difficult for people to relate to such an abstraction. We need a sense of divinity with whom we can interact. Jesus, God's son, plays that role in the Gospels; Chochmah, God's daughter, plays it in Proverbs:

> I fill the hearts of those who love me,
> they will never lack for insight.
> I am the deep grain of creation, the subtle current of life.
> God fashioned me before all things;
> I am the blueprint of creation.
> I was there from the beginning, from before there was a beginning.
> I am independent of time and space, earth and sky.
> I was before depth was conceived,
> before springs bubbled with water,
> before the shaping of mountains and hills,
> before God fashioned the earth and its bounty,
> before the first dust settled on the land.
> When God prepared the heavens, I was there.
> When the circle of the earth was etched into the face of the deep,
>   I was there.
> When the stars and planets soared into their orbit,
> when the deepest oceans found their level
> and the dry land established the shores,
> I was there.
> I stood beside God as firstborn and friend.
> My nature is joy, and I gave God constant delight.
> Now that the world is inhabited, I rejoice in it.
> I will be your true delight if you will heed my teachings.
>   (PROVERBS 8:21–31)

The choice of personifying wisdom as a woman reflects the larger world in which Jewish wisdom literature emerged. Chochmah is the Jewish parallel to goddesses such as Isis, Ma'at, Ishtar, and Asherah. Of the four, the Egyptian Ma'at most closely matches Chochmah. Isis, while knowledgeable, is also deceitful; Ishtar is more a goddess of war than a source of wisdom; and Asherah is the mother of the gods, but not aligned with wisdom per se. Ma'at, on the other hand, represents order, balance, and justice, as does Chochmah.

In the twenty-fifth-century-BCE text *The Proverbs of Ptah-hotep* (see Christian Jacq, *The Living Wisdom of Ancient Egypt* [New York: Simon & Schuster, 1999]), we learn that Ma'at, "Justice," is the foundation of creation (1.6, 5), and she alone endures (1.6, 7). Aligning with Ma'at ensures long life for both you and your children (1.18, 1). We can see parallels with Chochmah: she too was the foundation of creation (Proverbs 8:23); walking Chochmah's path is the key to a righteous and long life (Proverbs 2:20–22). In the Egyptian hymn to Amon-Re, the Egyptian creator and sustainer of life, Ma'at is revealed as Truth who comes forth from Amon-Re and burns up the wicked. Proverbs 2:20–22 tells that Chochmah comes from God and cuts off and uproots the wicked.

Another influence on the creation of Lady Wisdom may be the seventh-century-BCE text the *Proverbs of Ahiqar*. Written in Aramaic in northern Syria, Ahiqar tells us that Wisdom is "of the gods. Indeed she is precious to the gods; Her kingdom is [eternal]. She has been established by *Samayn* [lord of heaven]; Yea the Holy Lord has exalted her" (James M. Lindenberger, *The Aramaic Proverbs of Ahiqar* [Baltimore: Johns Hopkins University Press, 1983], pp. 19–20).

Chochmah was not simply the first of God's creations; she is, as *Bereshit Rabbah*, the sixth-century collection of rabbinic commentary, tells us, the blueprint of creation itself. To know Wisdom is to know the nature of reality; to know Wisdom is to become wise. To become wise is to find happiness and peace: "Her way is pleasant, and all her paths are peace. She is a Tree of Life to those who embrace her, and those that cleave to her find happiness" (Proverbs 3:17–8).

This last claim is testable. You don't believe in Wisdom; rather, you engage with her. If your engagement with Wisdom leads to pleasantness and peace, then you have proof that her teachings are true.

The key to the awakening that is Wisdom is having a clear perception of reality. Wisdom does not lead you to this clarity; she is this clarity.

Imagine you wake up in the middle of the night to find a snake coiled at the end of your bed. You freeze in fear and spend the rest of the night awake, afraid, and frozen in place. As dawn bathes your bedroom in soft light, you suddenly realize that the "snake" is simply the belt you forgot to put away as you undressed the night before. The fear ends as quickly as it arose. Nothing has changed but the quality of your perception.

The Women of Proverbs

The Book of Proverbs speaks of two kinds of women: Lady Wisdom (Chochmah, as discussed above) and Lady Folly, the Strange Woman, or Woman of Estrangement. Both ladies live on the high ground, so you can't say Wisdom is closer to God or heaven than is Folly. Both are calling to humans. Both offer food, but the food of wisdom brings life and the food of folly brings death:

> Wisdom is not the only voice you will hear.
> Foolishness too has her house and her servants.
> She sits at the doorway of her house and flaunts ignorance as if it
>   were gold.
> Her servants also climb the city's towers and call out to you:
> To the simple they say: *Turn in here.*
> To those whose hearts are dry they say:
> *You think Wisdom's wine is sweet?*
> *My stolen water is even sweeter.*
> *You think Wisdom's feast is filling?*
> *Eat my bread in secret and your mouth will taste true pleasure.*
> Do you know she sleeps with corpses?
> Do you know her house is the gateway to the grave?
>
> (PROVERBS 9:13–18)

The two women of the Book of Proverbs, Wisdom and Folly, are offering you a choice: will you take the way of wisdom and life or the way of folly and death? This is the existential choice the Book of Proverbs sets before you. It is easy to say, "I will choose life," but doing so doesn't mean memorizing and spouting the proverbs of Lady Wisdom whenever the chance arises. It means dining with her and listening to her, and making her words a part of your very being so that they can over time transform your consciousness. It is not enough that you follow Wisdom; you must become wise yourself.

How to Read the Book of Proverbs

The Book of Proverbs isn't a *Bartlett's Familiar Quotations*. It isn't a collection of clever sayings for toastmasters. The sayings themselves have the power to transform the mind of the student. But they have to be entered into carefully. Just reciting a proverb is meaningless: "A parable from the lips of the ignorant is as useless as shoes on a man without legs" (Proverbs 26:7); "A thorn in the hand of a drunk causes as much trouble as a parable told by a fool" (Proverbs 26:9). I suggest you don't simply read Proverbs, but work with them the way a Zen Buddhist might work with a Zen koan.

Koans are puzzles given to students of Zen as a means to shatter the limits of the narrow mind (*mochin d'katnut*) and open to spacious mind (*mochin d'gadlut*). Narrow mind imagines you to be separate from the world and the One who manifests it. Narrow mind pits you against the world, convinced of a zero-sum reality in which your success depends on another's failure. Narrow mind is isolated, alienated, frightened, and ignorant of the truth. Spacious mind is the opposite.

Spacious mind realizes that all life is a manifestation of the singular dynamic of living; call it God, Reality, Heaven, Ground of Being, Tao, what have you. Realizing the unity of all things in, with, and as God, spacious mind is fearless, creative, compassionate, inclusive, and loving. Spacious mind offers a non-zero-sum worldview in which your success requires the success of others and cannot be achieved at their expense.

Narrow mind operates under the principle of self-sufficiency: it believes that it can and must function on its own. Since there is nothing "on its own" in the universe, all things being a manifestation of the One, narrow mind expends a lot of energy maintaining the illusion of its own isolation. Koans and the teachings in the Book of Proverbs bring this wall crumbling down.

To allow for such collapse you have to live with the proverb. You don't recite it as a mantra, but rather scratch at it as you might an unbearable itch. The more you scratch, the more it itches; the more it itches, the more you scratch. The proverb begins to take over your life, making it more and more difficult to maintain the walls of falsehood and foolishness in which the narrow mind is so very invested. In time, the walls crumble and you see what is so in fact rather than in fantasy.

As you read through the hundreds of teachings in this book, mark those that catch you up short. These are the teachings that, for whatever reason, start you itching. Now start scratching.

Write the proverb down in a small notebook, and carry it with you. Keep track of the insights revealed to you every time you make time to ponder the proverb anew. Eventually you won't need the notebook and will simply stop carrying it. At that point the proverb is no longer something you carry, but something that carries you: it is the lens through which you view the world, one that is incompatible with the lens of narrow mind. As you work with proverbs, the lens of narrow mind shatters and the more inclusive seeing of spacious mind becomes the norm. When this happens, take up another proverb, for the return of narrow mind is as natural to you as the breakthrough of spacious mind. There is no end to proverb practice, there is only the next proverb.

A Word on Translation

There are dozens of fine English translations of the Book of Proverbs. I offer my own not to compete with those that are already available but to complement them. While rooted in the original Hebrew, this translation seeks to reveal the deeper meaning of the text often lost in more conventional translations. Like all my translations (and I would suggest like all translations period), my version of the Book of Proverbs reflects my understanding of the meaning of the Hebrew, and not just the dictionary equivalent in English. The Book of Proverbs speaks to me in a personal and powerful way, and it is the message that I hear in these proverbs that I seek to make clear to you in my rendering of the Book of Proverbs. To see what I see in the Book of Proverbs, it is helpful to read my translation alongside more conventional renderings such as the New Revised Standard Version (NRSV) or the Jewish Publication Society translation (JPS).

A Word of Thanks

This is my ninth book with SkyLight Paths, all of which were written under the thoughtful guidance of my editor, Emily Wichland. Over the years Emily and I have developed a rhythm that goes something like this: I write, she questions, I complain, she waits, I realize her questions are opportunities for me to deepen my understanding of the text and the quality of my writing, I rewrite, she edits, I rewrite again, she approves, we are done. It is a creative dance in which I delight, and of which I never grow tired. Thanks to Emily and the entire SkyLight Paths family for this chance to share my love of yet another sacred text.

Proverbs

1 | While traditionally ascribed to Solomon, the language and phrasing of Proverbs reflect a period long after his death. Saying these are the proverbs of Solomon is to say they reflect the best wisdom of their day.

2 | The wise teach through parable, puzzle, and proverb. Their words point to something beyond themselves. For those who read only the surface, who take the words as merely words, there is guidance; but to those who see the words not as signs but as symbols, not as points of fact but pointers to the unknown, these teachings are so much more.

3 | The Hebrew here is *yirat Adonai* (sometimes rendered as *yirat HaShem*, referring to the Name [*HaShem*] of God), most often translated as "fear of the Lord." *Yirah* also means "wonder and awe," and *Adonai* (Lord) is a late Rabbinic euphemism for the ineffable Name of God, *Yod-Heh-Vav-Heh*, which is not a noun at all but a form of the Hebrew verb "to be." God is what is, and the process of "be-ing" itself. You do not "fear" this process; you *are* this process. God is you the way an ocean is a wave. The proper response to this realization is a sense of awe that temporarily erases your sense of otherness, your egoic "I." Solomon is telling you that there is a way to this nondual awareness, and it is this awareness that is both the foundation of wisdom and its fruit.

4 | The wisdom of Proverbs is both a what and a way. That is to say, the sayings themselves reflect not only the knowledge to be gained but also the way to gain it. It is not enough to know these sayings intellectually; you must embody them physically.

☐ The Nine Foundational Teachings

Introduction

1:1–7
These are the proverbs and parables of Solomon, son of
    David, king of Israel;[1]
A guide to insight, understanding, and spiritual discipline
to help you become generous, honest, and balanced.
They are offered to the simple that they may gain
    knowledge;
to the young that they may find direction;
to the learned that they might peer behind the words and
    attain wisdom,
for I speak in riddles both simple and profound,
wise words that hide deeper meanings.[2]

Begin with this: The foundation of wisdom is the selfless awe
    of God.[3]
Skeptics deny that this is so, and the ignorant refuse the
    discipline that achieves it,
but you need not be among them.[4]

5 You are both seeker and thief, and you must learn to choose between them. The seeker is that inner impulse toward *echad*—unity, nonduality, the realization that self and other, wave and ocean, you and God are all one. The thief is the inner impulse toward *achad*—separation and alienation. It robs you of peace and tranquility by trapping you in a false world of endless craving and competition. The thief says there is an empty sack to be filled. The sack is the feeling of aloneness and alienation that arises from ignorance. The thief says it can be filled by stuffing yourself with things, ideas, illusions, and pride. The thief lies. There is no sack of *achad*; there is only the reality of *echad*. The wisdom that comes from the sage is the realization that there is no sack to fill, only a divine reality to be realized and lived.

6 The trap the thief lays promises an end to *achad*, alienation; the wisdom of the sage promises no less. They differ in means, not promised ends. The way of the thief is like one who seeks to fill a bucket with seawater by running back and forth between the bucket and the sea carrying water in scooped hands. The way of the sage is like one who fills the bucket by tossing it into the sea itself. The way of the thief is exhausting and ultimately fruitless. The way of the sage is effortless and instantaneous. You know you are following the way of the thief if you are exhausted by your search for meaning, purpose, God, and godliness.

The First Teaching

1:8–19

You are guided from the very beginning:
The instruction of your father—do not abandon it!
The teaching of your mother—do not forsake it!
Let their discipline adorn you as a necklace and crown,
so that you do not fall victim to foolish desires,
who, like thieves, lay in ambush for the innocent.[5]
They call to you: *Come, join us. We will murder the weak and fill our homes with their wealth and dignity; there will be a single pouch for us all.*
Do not set your feet on their path, for it leads only to self-destruction.
They rush to violence, driven by a jealous hunger, never satisfied.
When you go forth to trap a bird, what do you do?
You spread grain to lure it in.
The bird takes the grain; you take the bird.
When evil seeks to entrap you, it does the same.
Desire takes the place of grain, and you are no smarter than the bird.
The trap looks so innocent, yet its endless yearning exhausts both body and soul.[6]

(continued on page 7)

7   Wisdom—*Chochmah* in Hebrew, *Sophia* in Greek—is personified as a woman. This is more than an accident of grammar. As we shall see in Proverb 8, Chochmah is the daughter of God, both the map and the means of creation. Wisdom is the way God is God in the world you and I encounter. To know the world is to know Wisdom, and to know Wisdom is to know God. Chochmah does away with the false split between science and religion. True science—the humble and humbling exploration of the way things are—is true Wisdom, the way of all things. Chochmah is both the discovered and the discoverer, both the way to and the way of truth. While it is true that the reality revealed by Chochmah encompasses dimensions beyond the material focus of the physical sciences, there is nothing in the way of science that is not part of the Way of Wisdom.

8   The way of trouble is the way of I–It, the way of exploiting others in the service of one self. The way of truth is the way of I–Thou, the way of interdependence and harmony. Why choose trouble over truth? Because the one sustains your sense of *achad*, separateness, even uniqueness, while the other humbles you to the point of dissolution in the reality of *echad*, nonduality. It is frightening to know that you are not unique, that you are a knot in the network of God's creation rather than a separate net all your own. Fear of selflessness maintains the false self.

1.20 33

How different it is with Wisdom!
She lays no snares and has no need to hide.
She sings openly in the street;
she speaks clearly,
her voice rising above the tumult of the market and the gates
    of the city.
It is one thing if a child surrenders to desire,
but when adults act childishly, it is true folly.
You will never outgrow the snare of cynicism and
    foolishness.
You are never too old for wickedness.
You can resist Wisdom's words all your life,
yet, she will never give up on you.[7]

Wisdom speaks deep within you, saying:
I will continue to share my spirit with you.
I will speak my truth, though you refuse to hear me.
I will stretch forth my hand though you slap it away.
I will offer counsel though you plug your ears.
I will not laugh, knowing that all your dramas are born of ignorance.
I will remain compassionate even as you choose trouble over truth.[8]

(continued on page 9)

9 While Wisdom calls to you continually, the habit of stuffing your ears and muting her call can, over time, make her seem lost. After a lifetime of self-absorption it is nearly impossible to move beyond the self. You are like a person wandering lost in a canyon calling for help and hearing only the echo of your own voice calling back to you, drowning out the voices of those searching for you.

10 Tranquility is the hallmark of Wisdom. It is not that the wise possess a body of knowledge that others do not. It is that they embody this knowledge in ways that others do not. The fool may hear the teaching of nonduality, and even understand it intellectually, and yet reject it as a guiding principle for living life. It isn't that they cannot know the truth, it is that they do not live the truth. The wise hear and live, and the sign of their living is a tranquility that arises not from detachment to what is but from surrendering to the way things are.

Yet even I have limits, and I worry that I will tire and withdraw.
Then when fearsome darkness swallows you and
misfortune overtakes you,
when your body fails you and your spirit flags,
when at last you call out: Wisdom, please reveal yourself to me!
I will be too weak to respond.
When you finally come in search of Me, I may be too lost to be found.[9]

If you hate knowledge and spurn wisdom;
if you reject my counsel and refuse my direction,
all you have left is the bitter fruit of your own orchards,
the emptiness of your own schemes.
Your own recklessness will kill you, a homicide at the hand
of desire.
Listen to me and my words will protect you;
heed me and you can face your strongest desires with
tranquility.[10]

11 Single-mindedness has two meanings here. First, it carries the notion of focus: nothing matters more to you than the pursuit of wisdom. Second, it hints at the truth of nonduality. The world is a single process perceivable only when the mind is single, that is, when it is in a state of *echad* rather than *achad*, unity rather than alienation.

12 A mind at one with the One is in a state of awe and wonder, what the Hebrew original calls *yirat,* and what many translators render as "fear." Fear, however, requires a self to be afraid and an "other" to be afraid of. In the state of awe and wonder both self and other dissolve into the greater nonduality that is God alone.

13 The attentive are those who are mindful of the present moment. The ancient Rabbis often spoke of God as *HaMakom*, "the Place," referring to God as both the place in which you stand and the larger place in which all place rests. The attentive know their place to be a manifestation of God.

14 Life is complex but not complicated. Complexity is part of nature: processes interacting with one another in the greater context of life and living. Complications arise only when you seek to bend reality to your will. Or, to put this more poetically: life is complex when you know God is playing you; life is complicated when you play at being God. The simple are those at home with complexity but not in love with complication.

The Second Teaching

2:1–8

Will you heed my words and accept my direction?

Then open your ears to wisdom and incline your heart to
clarity.

Call on understanding, a trusted mother whose love is all
you need.

Seek her single-mindedly as though she were a hidden
treasure.[11]

Only wonder reveals the grandeur and grace of God.[12]

God is unbounded wisdom, knowledge, and insight.

Wisdom upon wisdom, God is the foundation of truth.

Only the attentive will find God,[13] only the simple will know
truth;[14]

and God will grant these to you, safeguarding the paths of
justice

and protecting those who choose to walk them.

(continued on page 13)

15 Wisdom is not an idea to be known, but a life path to be lived. The wise are no less committed to righteousness, justice, and fairness than they are to wisdom. In fact, the more wise they become, the more righteously, justly, and fairly they live. These traits along with tranquility are the hallmarks of the wise.

16 The complexity of life embraces a multiplicity of processes and paths. While one might say life is a journey from birth to death, that journey encompasses a variety of smaller journeys. The foolish impose upon themselves, and often others as well, consistency that isn't natural to life, a straight path that denies the natural crookedness of life. The wise have no fear of the crooked and bent and calmly walk whatever path is presented to them, knowing that all paths are part of the way.

17 Each of us has a shadow side, a part of us that is shrouded in darkness and pain and that we all too often project onto others. The way of Wisdom is through the shadow; it brings light to the dark places of our lives so that we are not fooled into believing our own madness and imagining that we are light and projecting onto others all that is dark in us and fearful.

2:9–13

When wisdom is embraced, righteousness, justice, and
 fairness are known;[15]
all paths are illumined and you need fear no detour.[16]
When wisdom enters your heart and knowledge your soul,
you will perceive the order of the universe and never despair.
You will be rescued from your own dark inclinations, and
not even the cleverest lies will fool you.[17]

(continued on page 15)

18 Evil is as natural to life as good. Wisdom doesn't end evil any more than up puts an end to down, or right puts an end to left. Rather, Wisdom illumes the way so that good and evil are clear to you and you can choose the former without fear of accidently falling into the latter. Walking with Wisdom is like walking in a dark house with a flashlight: while there are plenty of things to bump into and fall over, your flashlight allows you to navigate around them safely.

19 The Book of Proverbs speaks of two kinds of feminine force: one leads to wisdom, the other to despair. They are both spoken of as women because they refer to the inner workings of spirit that, in Hebrew, are feminine forces, while the outer world of the body is considered masculine. This is not to be confused with men and women. This speaks to body and soul. The lifeless feminine are those forces that reduce both self and other to the status of It, objects to be exploited and abused. In this world there is no loyalty or love, only cheapened pleasures sold at exorbitant prices.

20 Having a home means having a sense of place, *makom*. The home of the wise is *HaMakom*, the Divine Place embracing and transcending all places. The home of the fool is no less (for there is no place outside of God), but because they insist on treating themselves and others as objects, they rush from place to place seeking that which can only be found when they shift from the world of It to the world of Thou. They are like people racing from room to room searching for home without ever realizing they are already and always home.

2:14–22

Wisdom rescues you from evil[18]
and saves you from the snare of empty pleasure and lies.
She keeps you from those whose paths are false and lifeless,
who find joy in doing evil
and take pleasure in causing suffering.

She keeps you from those who sell physical pleasure for profit
and those who love without loyalty.
They walk a lifeless way;
and to follow them is to live as if dead.[19]

Choose differently: seek wisdom and walk the good path.
The upright dwell in timeless wisdom;
the wholehearted can never be lost,
but the wicked are driven from every place and
the faithless have nowhere to call home.[20]

21　There are many realms to reality, many dimensions from the smallest quark to the largest quasar. All of them are the manifestations of Chochmah, the body of God expressed in the world we know and can know. And there are dimensions beyond our knowing, dimensions that can be tapped, not by the "I" of ego, the "I" that knows, but only by the *ehyeh* of God, the I that knows no other, the I that is Thou. These divine realms of greater and greater inclusivity can, if we are open to them, stream insight and compassion into the realms we can know. The I of God can touch the I of self and provide a glimpse of liberating insight that we might know that we are not what we think, but the One doing the thinking.

22　The Hebrew I render as "just" is *y'yashayr,* literally, "he will straighten." This should be understood as being morally straight, upright, and just rather than the idea that God will straighten out the curves and bumps of your life. Life is anything but straight. Yet no matter how many twists and turns your life path may take, you can walk that path justly, uprightly, doing good and bringing justice to bear with every step.

23　The life Wisdom reveals is not zero-sum; your success is not dependent upon another's failure. Knowing that success comes from the Infinite One, you no longer have to fear that another's success somehow means there is less for you. Knowing that giving is infinite leads you to give as well. You discover yourself to be a vehicle for blessing rather than a silo hoarding blessings for yourself.

24　The gift is always the same: this moment. The teaching is always the same: this moment. Do not look for something other than what is; know that what is, is what must be, and your task is to engage it with compassion, grace, and justice.

The Third Teaching

3:1–4
Remember my teaching and
and observe my precepts.
My words will bless your years with tranquility and peace.
Let kindness and truth adorn you, speak of them often,
inscribe them on the tablets of your heart that they shape
   your every thought.
Do this and you are beloved in realms both human and
   divine.[21]

3:5–12
Do not make a crutch of ego, lean on God alone.
Adhere to the good and your path will be just.[22]
Do not imagine that you are wise.
Know only that you do not know.
Stand in awe of the Infinite and turn away from evil.
In this way you strengthen both body and soul.
Know from Whom success comes and give generously to
   those in need.[23]
Your wealth will increase as a result of your generosity;
none can fathom the rewards of those who share their
   wealth.
Not everything that happens will be enjoyable,
and not every word you hear will be kind,
yet receive everything as a gift and a teaching.[24]

(continued on page 19)

25 It is important not to read this to mean that the wise never know grief or suffer discontent. These are as much a part of life for the wise as for the foolish. The difference is that the wise do not expect things to be other than they are. They understand that the complexity of life means that conditions will arise now and again that necessitate grief and suffering. These they will accept with the same tranquility as their opposites—joy and well-being. The wise know that they are not intended beneficiaries of good nor the intended targets of evil. They are simply part of the complexity of life unfolding this way and that according to the conditions of the moment—conditions over which the wise know they have no control.

What separates the wise and the foolish is that the wise expect only what is and accept reality as it is, learning how to navigate life in all its forms with tranquility, grace, compassion, and peace, while the foolish expect only what they desire and rail against life when it offers what they do not desire, and thus live in a hell of unfulfilled desire.

26 In Genesis we are told that Adam is expelled from the Garden because he eats from this very tree, yet Wisdom is this tree and the wise are to embrace her. The change is in the state of Adam, humanity. In the Garden, Adam ate from the Tree of Knowledge of Good and Evil, the Tree of Opposites, and felt fear and shame. Those who follow Wisdom realize that all opposites are from a greater Wholeness and move beyond fear to awe and beyond shame to wonder. Having made that shift, they return to the Garden, to that state of wholeness and peace, and embrace the Tree of Life, finding in Wisdom the key to timeless tranquility.

27 Why is Wisdom a Tree of Life? Because she is the foundation of life. Wisdom is the current of the sea as well as the water; she is the grain of jade as well as the rock. To know Wisdom is to know the way of all things, and to know the way of all things is to know the way of the self and that Source from which self and all things arise.

3:13–20

Only the wise are happy, for they deal in wisdom,
whose value exceeds silver and gold,
and whose preciousness is greater than pearls.
Wisdom is the way to everlasting life, true wealth, and honor.
Her way is pleasant, and all her paths are peace.[25]
She is a Tree of Life to those who embrace her,
and those that cleave to her find happiness.[26]
Wisdom is the foundation of the earth, and
understanding the pillar of sky.
A divine order patterns all of creation,
from the timeless ocean to the fleeting dew.[27]

(continued on page 21)

28 The way of Wisdom is not other than the way of nature. Observing the patterns of life, standing in awe before the grandeur of the cosmos, places you in that state of mind where, as poet William Blake wrote in *Augaries of Innocence*, you see the infinite in a single grain of sand. Wisdom does not ask you to leave this world for some other, but to see this world as a manifestation of a larger reality that embraces and transcends it. In short, celebrating *achad* as a manifestation of *echad* rather than as an end in and of itself.

29 Sleep is fearful and waking is anxious because we know we have no control over either. The "I" of ego, the *achad* without *echad*, craves control like a drug addict craves the next fix. But there is no control. This is the key to tranquility that the wise have attained. They do not seek to control their lives, only to master their response to life. What happens, happens; but how we respond to what happens is up to us.

30 Once awake to truth, the wise cannot fall back into delusion. Once you know that the snake in the corner of the room is not a snake at all, but a coil of rope, you cannot pretend otherwise. Wisdom banishes fear by shining a light on the dark corners of illusion.

3:21–26
Keep your attention on wisdom,
and do not allow yourself to be distracted.
Watch the patterns of creation.
This will enliven your soul and bring you grace and
tranquility.[28]
Seeing truth you can walk forward in confidence
without stumbling because of ignorance.
When you sleep you will not be afraid;
your sleep will come easily.
When you wake you will not be anxious[29]
nor worry about your fate,
for you rest safely in the divine
and your feet do not stray from the path.[30]

(continued on page 23)

31 This is the outer way of the wise. They give when asked, sow no evil, and never betray a trust. They waste no time arguing with fools and are not drawn toward violence.

32 Intimacy requires overcoming both self and other and entering into a greater oneness. This is something the wise know and desire, and something that the foolish deny and reject. This is why only the wise are intimate with God. The foolish are no less part of the Divine Whole, but their addiction to *achad*, alienation and their own sense of sovereign self, preclude them from being surrendered into the embrace of God.

33 You become that with which you associate. You become like those with whom you bind. Seek out a community of the wise; bind yourself to those who live the way of *echad* and I–Thou, and you will find in them mirrors to your own realization.

3:27–35
Do not hold back from helping others;
share what you have without reservation.
Do not say to the needy: *Ask me again tomorrow*,
when you can do something today.
Do not sow seeds of evil or betray those who trust you.
Do not quarrel even with those who do not have your best
    interests at heart.
Do not envy the violent or imitate them,
for one who strays from the path of peace turns away from
    all that is holy;[31]
only the upright are intimate with God.[32]
The houses of the wicked are condemned, but the homes of
    the just are blessed.
Do not underestimate the power of association:
align yourself with scoffers and you will scoff;[33]
practice humility and you will be appreciated.
The wise inherit honor, the legacy of the fool is disgrace.

34 Wisdom is gleaned through mindfulness. She is the way things are. When you attend carefully to what is happening, you attend to Wisdom, for she is what is happening, and how it is happening, and in this way you begin to understand the way of all things.

35 Wisdom protects you and keeps you safe, but do not mistake her safety for a life without challenge, suffering, or doubt. Wisdom is the way of reality, and reality includes challenge, suffering, and doubt. There is no way to avoid difficulties, there is only a way to engage them. When you understand the way of Wisdom, you understand that each moment is to be embraced without resistance; accepting what is, is the only way to impact what is to come. In other words, Wisdom doesn't help you avoid the punches, but teaches you how to roll with them.

36 Wisdom offers no process or technique. Life is the process; living is the technique. Wisdom does not say, "Pray this way, or meditate that way, and you will find me." Rather she says, "Here I am. And here. And here again. I am what is happening at this very moment. Attend to me. Embrace me. Love and accept me without fear and hesitation. Imagine a person suddenly tossed into the sea. If she struggles, she drowns. If she surrenders, she is buoyed. Surrender to what is; surrender to me, and I will do the same."

The Fourth Teaching

4:1–6

Listen and attend, and understanding will follow.[34]
You have been given a good teaching; don't abandon it.
When I was young, beloved of my parents,
my father taught me:
Let my words sustain your heart;
practice my discipline and live.
Do not forsake Wisdom, and she will protect you;
love her and she will keep you safe.[35]

4:7–9

What is the beginning of wisdom? Get wisdom![36]
Whatever else you do, get insight.
Praise her and she will lift you up.
Embrace her and she will honor you.
She will circle your brow like a fresh garland
and rest on your mind as a crown upon your head.

(continued on page 27)

37 Solomon returns again to the walk of the wise. It is a recurring metaphor in Proverbs, reminding you that wisdom is a way, a path, and one that is walked without fear, hesitation, or stumbling. This is because the way of the wise is illumined by Wisdom.

38 What is the practice of wisdom? It isn't a set technique, but rather a specific attitude rooted in insight and understanding of the nonduality of life. You practice living as *echad* rather than *achad* (one with rather than separate from life). You see the world as *echad* rather than *achad* (a single complex and dynamic whole rather than a series of independent parts). Each moment, regardless of what it brings, is an opportunity to say, "Yes, this too is of God."

39 Just as nature embraces a spectrum of possibilities from a gentle rain to a devastating hurricane, so human nature embraces a spectrum of possibilities from saint to psychopath. Don't be deluded into thinking that because everyone is God, everyone is good. God is not to be reduced to good. God is reality. This is the wisdom that Wisdom reveals. Accept the fact that there are people whose only desire is to harm. Avoid them when you can; defeat them when you must.

40 It is simple to tell who is wise and who is wicked. The former diminish darkness; the latter spread it.

4:10–19

I have instructed you in wisdom, and set before you the way
of tranquility.

When you walk, walk freely, secure in the knowledge that
you will not stray.

When you run, run effortlessly, knowing that your foot will
not stumble.[37]

Be diligent in your practice and do not abandon it.
Keep it dear to you, for it is life itself.
Do not nurse doubts and schemes;
and if they arise, do not invite them in.
Reject the temptation to do evil,
and do not daydream of revenge.[38]

There are fools who cannot rest until they have done
another harm;
evil fools who cannot sleep until they have caused another to
fall.
Evil is their life bread, and violence their wine.[39]

The path of the wise is like the sun at dawn,
illumining more of the world as the day lengthens into noon.
But the way of the fool is a thickening darkness,
and their every step fearful and uncertain.[40]

(continued on page 29)

41 There is an intimacy implied here. Inclining your ear means moving closer to the mouth of your teacher, trusting that the words are worthy of your trust. Wisdom is taught from sage to student in a relationship not unlike that of parent and child. But you are not a child, and you must hold your teacher to the standards of the teaching, making no excuses for behavior that violates the path being taught.

42 It is because of this that you must protect your heart. Don't allow your love for the teaching to be mistaken for love for your teacher. Wisdom frees the heart, but there are many masquerading as wise who only wish to entrap it.

43 While there is much to learn from the past, there is no point in living in it. Wisdom is about moving forward, embracing what is next, and setting it aside when the next moment arises. This is the straight path: not a way without detour, but one without regret.

4:20–27

Listen carefully to me, my child; incline your ear to my
    teaching.[41]
Train your eyes to see Wisdom, and your heart to shelter her.
These teachings give life to those who find them
and are a balm to the body of those who embrace them.
Protect your heart above all else,
for the heart determines the quality of your life.[42]

Free yourself from hateful speech;
put aside all duplicitous talk.
Rest your eyes on the horizon,
and let your vision focus on what is next.[43]
Keep your feet on the upright path.
Do not waver to the right or to the left;
and turn your foot away from the path of evil.

44 The desire you are warned against here is the desire rooted in self that leads to selfishness. This is a desire that excuses the exploitation of others in the pursuit of personal wants.

45 The "two" is the false sense of self and other that pits self against other. In truth, there is no separate self. There is only a singular reality manifesting here as "this" and there as "that."

46 The way of desire is the way of separation and alienation, leaving you feeling isolated and fearful. This feeling leaves you incapable of joy, and life without joy is death.

The Fifth Teaching

5:1–6
Attend now to my words,
incline your ear to grasp my meaning.
Express your thoughts with wisdom and your words with
    truth.
Yet even then the sweet honey of desire will tempt you.[44]
Slippery as oil is the way of desire.
Taste this honey and your lips swell with bitterness;
follow this path and a double-edged desire will cleave you in
    two.[45]
The way of desire leads only to the grave; the path itself is
    death.[46]

Make no comparison between these two paths, for that
    legitimizes them both.
Do not imagine that they offer you a choice, for that sets
    you at a crossroad.
The wise do not ask which is the true path; their feet are
    naturally drawn to it.

(*continued on page 33*)

47 Choice arises only when your view of reality is clouded. When you see the fire in front of you, do you choose not to walk into it, or does the option of self-immolation never come to mind? When you see the truth, you will always act in accordance with it.

48 The heart here doesn't mean the seat of emotions, but the seat of wisdom. The heart reveals the interdependence of all life, and knowing that unity makes the bitterness of imagined alienation disappear.

49 Succumbing to desire is succumbing to selfishness and the false view that the self exists separate from the whole.

50 There is much you can learn from others, but always test what you learn against your own experience. The wisdom of a teacher is not to be followed blindly, but tested in the caldron of your own life.

5:7–11

So avoid comparison and the illusion of choice.[47]

Abide in your heart,[48] for without this connection each year
   is more bitter than the next.

Succumb to desire[49] and all your treasure will be lost;

your body will tire from worry;

your soul consumed by doubt, and your heart brittle as glass.

Your final days will be plagued with self-criticism,

and your last moments haunted by regret.

Your final thoughts will be cries of despair:

How could I have hated discipline, and turned a deaf ear to my teachers?

*How could I have ignored wisdom's promise and surrendered to fleeting
   pleasure?*

5:12–19

Yet do not put your trust in teachers alone.[50]

Drink their deep store of wisdom,

but seek out also water from your own well.

Do this and the thirsty will come to you, saying:

Our souls are parched, our hearts like baked leather;

give us a sip of your water to help us revive.

This wisdom is yours alone, unclouded by others' words and
   schemes.

The source of your wisdom is blessedness.

Drink it and experience the joy of a lover's first kiss.

As mountain goats run to each other, so will others run to you.

You will nurse them with the milk of wisdom,

and both of you will be drunk on love.

(continued on page 35)

51 Desire's power comes from her promise to fill you with life. Her breasts appear full, but it is dust that fills them. The milk of love and compassion is not found in the breast of desire, only in the breast of wisdom.

52 Do not imagine that others determine what happens to you. Your deeds in this moment set the stage for what you will encounter in the next moment. This doesn't mean good begets good or evil begets evil, but that good strengthens your capacity to embrace with compassion and tranquility whatever life brings.

5:20–23

Be not seduced by desire.

She promises nourishment, but her breast is dry.[51]

Align your deeds with godliness,

for your actions alone determine your fate—[52]

sin leads only to sin;

despair brings only despair;

the sands of delusion will swirl around you,

and you will be blind to truth;

you will die and what wisdom you had will evaporate in the
hot wind.

53 The Book of Proverbs finds wisdom in nature rather than revelation. Look to the ant rather than the Hebrew Bible! This is what makes the Book of Proverbs and the rest of the biblical wisdom literature unique: life will show you how best to live.

54 Wisdom is a discipline. While the gift of wisdom is your birthright, that is, while you are born with the capacity to become wise, you have to develop that capacity through disciplined observation.

The Sixth Teaching

6:1–5

Remember what promises you make. Do not pledge to one
    and then make a conflicting promise to another.
In this way your mouth becomes a snare and your words
    trap you.
If this occurs, go to the first and humble yourself.
Do not rest or sleep until you have done what you can to set
    the matter right.

6:6–11

Do you need a model for your actions? Look to the ant!
Adopt her way of life and grow wise.
No one gives her instructions,
yet she prepares her food in summer and gathers her grain at
    harvest time.
She does what is right for herself and does not steal from
    others.[53]

Do not be lazy about the work of wisdom,
hiding in your bed, asleep to the knowledge that is your
    birthright.
The dawn comes and you groan:
Just a bit more sleep, a few more minutes;
let me tuck my hand under my head and
close my eyes for a little while longer.
And what happens while you dawdle?
Poverty of spirit overtakes you,
and sloth blocks your way like a shield.[54]

(continued on page 39)

55 The way of Wisdom should not be mistaken for the way that comes naturally. Left to your own selfish devices, you will seek to exploit others for your own ends, and end up leaving yourself open to exploitation by others. The unwise self is selfish and fearful. The wise self acts for the good of the whole of which it is a part, feeling no fear from another, because it sees all others are part of itself. This realization is not alien to you, but most often so buried within you that only disciplined searching can uncover it.

56 These are the seven acts of selfishness that make wisdom and wise action impossible. Do the opposite of these and you are disciplining yourself in wisdom for Wisdom: cultivate humility rather than arrogance, honesty rather than deceit, kind thoughts rather than hateful ones, generosity rather than hoarding, avoidance of hurtful acts rather than an eager pursuit of them, a simple observing mind rather than one obsessed with taking advantage of others' weaknesses, a gentle mind rather than one bound to violence.

6:12–15

Without self-discipline you are enslaved to desire,
and every word you utter promotes a scheme.
You wink at the truth and cause others to doubt.
You feign humility as a ploy to spread evil gossip.
You point a finger of blame and sully the reputation of the
   blameless.
Your innermost thoughts are corrupt;
your mind says *yes* when your heart pleads *no*.
Your every desire is for exploitation.
You delight in setting friends at odds.
You are so intent on bringing misfortune to others,
your own situation goes unnoticed
and evil catches you unaware.
It deals you a fatal blow.[55]

6:16–19

Six things cut you off from the holy,
a seventh makes even your soul a monster:
an arrogant manner, a deceitful tongue, murderous thoughts,
a thieving heart, feet eager to run after evil, a scheming mind,
and a tendency to arouse violence in those who once lived in
   peace.[56]

(continued on page 41)

57 The wisdom the Book of Proverbs promotes is a way of action: deeds of justice and compassion. It is not a way of knowing only, but a way of knowing in the service of doing.

58 Lamps without flames are dark shells. Flames without lamps to sustain them are mere flashes. The two must come together. Wisdom informs your deeds, and your deeds sustain your wisdom.

6:20–22

Do not forget the rules of justice
or the subtle teachings of compassion.[57]
Bind your heart with them
and tie them as a scarf around your neck
that whatever comes out of your mouth is tempered by
    goodness.
Do this and they will guide your steps;
your sleep will be dreamless, your waking free from guilt;
and Wisdom will speak with you like a close friend.

6:23–26

Deeds are lamps, and wisdom the flame that lights them.[58]
Learn from your mistakes; there is no shame in error.
Close your mouth to gossip, and your ear to falsehood.
How lovely is desire; do not be tempted by it.
How attractive its promise; do not be seduced by its charms.
For desire will steal your wisdom
and force you to beg for a slice of bread when whole loaves
    are your due.
Your life is precious; do not sacrifice it to evil.

(continued on page 43)

59 Desire is natural to life; selfishness cannot be separated from self. But this does not mean you must succumb to desire and selfishness, only that you must be aware of them. And if you do fall victim to desire, do not pretend otherwise. Admit your mistake, make what amends you can, and move on.

6:27–35

Even the firewalker's feet are sometimes scorched by hot
    coals.
How can your heart not burn when walking the path of
    desire?
There is desire in all of us, and none can escape it;
you may not root it out, but you can rein it in.
If you are caught stealing because you are hungry,
the judge will understand; pay what you owe and depart.
But there is no mercy for those who deliberately inflame the
    heart.
Their souls are crushed, they are humiliated,
and their disgrace is never-ending.
The flame of truth engulfs them
and no one pities them.
There is no ransoming of the wicked,
and justice is not thwarted by bribes.[59]

60 Who is the speaker here? Wisdom, herself. Again, note the absence of the God found in the Hebrew Bible and the Prophets. The way of Wisdom is its own path and not another reframing of the religion of Moses. Wisdom's words are the key to life, not the commandments (*mitzvot*) given to Moses.

61 Yet the result of both systems, the way of Wisdom and the way of Moses, is the same: compassion and justice. The difference is that the former is offered to the world, while the latter concerns itself with the Jews.

62 Wisdom is the mother of understanding. Wisdom in this case means intuitive insight, while understanding means rational processing of that insight. You can have no new thought without wisdom. Reason alone feeds on itself.

63 Evil is with us from our youth, but we only fall prey to it when we allow ourselves to be enticed by evil's allure. The allure of evil is the uplifting of self over others. When we fail to see the unity embracing and birthing all reality, we imagine ourselves apart from rather than a part of the whole. In this imagining, we fall prey to zero-sum thinking: for me to win, you must lose. Evil finds its way into our lives when we fall prey to the false notion that the victory of self is at the expense of the defeat of others.

The Seventh Teaching

7:1–5

Listen to me and treasure my instruction.

My words are the key to life; without them all you have is existence.[60]

Just as you shield your eyes from the sun so as not to be blinded,

these words will shield your heart from desire and protect your wisdom.

Tie them like a string on your finger to remind you of righteousness.

Align your heart with mercy, and your head with justice,[61]

so that your hand does what is right.

Call wisdom your sister, and understanding your niece,

for the latter is born of the former.[62]

Stay close to them and neither envy nor lust will distract you from the good.

7:6–8

I have looked through the lattice of the heart and

seen the ways of undisciplined desire.

The simple and the young are easy prey, for they lack self-control.

Yet do not imagine that they are innocent,

for evil cannot enter without our consent.[63]

Even young people must approach the threshold of desire

before evil can push them through the door.

(continued on page 47)

64 Wisdom reveals that you are part of the Whole and hence empowered by it. Without wisdom, you wrongfully imagine you are apart from the Whole and powerless. The quest for power over others rather than the realization that power arises from your unity with others is the way evil infects your life.

65 Evil never presents itself as evil, but always as good. The way you tell evil from wisdom isn't by their mutual claims of righteousness, but in how they treat self and other. Wisdom raises both; evil always prefers to raise the self at the other's expense.

66 There comes a point in succumbing to evil desire that you realize it is evil that has you in its grip, but it is too late to wrest yourself free. It is not that you lack the power, but that you lack the will. You want too strongly what evil offers so freely. And yet you know what you are about to do is wrong. The only comfort you have is in lying to yourself: I will change my ways if Wisdom returns. But it isn't Wisdom who has left you, but you who have abandoned her. There is no return of Wisdom when your own turning is toward evil.

7:9–20
Without wisdom you walk in perpetual twilight;
seeing only shadows and understanding little.
You are prey to evil desires.
Seductively dressed, they brazenly call you;
your heartbeat quickens with anticipation,
and thoughts of power race through your mind.[64]
Loud and demanding, they hound you.
You recognize them in the dark corners of your heart.
You feel their kisses on your mouth and you tremble with desire.
They thrust their faces up against our own and whisper:
Do not think us evil, we come simply to make peace, to lead you toward
   the good.
That is why we have arrived. This is why we are offering you this chance.
And, besides, how could we have found you unless God wanted us to?
Why should you give up the pleasures of the world?[65]
They draw you into bed; cover you in the softest Egyptian
   linen;
your head spins from their perfume—myrrh, aloes, and cinnamon.
They call to you sweetly:
Come, enjoy yourself until the grave beckons.
If you must repent, do it then.
Do you still think God cares about you and your world?
Look how the evil prosper! They find joy in every desire. Why don't you?
The righteous God kills mercilessly; why would you choose to be a victim?
Your wisdom is overturned,
your understanding is lost,
and the fear of sin is drowned out by desire.
Wisdom is lost no matter how frantically you seek her.
And you succumb, saying: *I will make amends if she returns.*[66]

(continued on page 49)

67 As horrible as this sounds, it is hopeful nonetheless. Giving into evil now doesn't mean you are doomed to evil forever. The pain your actions will cause you (as well as others) will eventually be so great as to make your continued allegiance to evil impossible. Eventually, you will be so sick of yourself and your deeds that you will repent and turn toward Wisdom once again.

68 Remember, Wisdom isn't a set of rules, but a guiding principle rooted in unity, compassion, and justice. When Wisdom tells you to defend yourself against evil by letting Wisdom reign in your heart, she is saying that as long as you rest in the compassion that arises from knowing the unity and interdependence of all things, you will not act out the selfish desires that arise within you. It is not the desire that will destroy you, but acting upon it.

7:21–23

You cannot withstand such seduction,
temptation's logic is inexorable.
It will lead you as an ox to the slaughter;
it is your own thoughts that lead you, there is no one else to
   blame.
Like a poisonous snake striking the heel of the careless,
like a sheep trotting mindlessly into the snare,
you will stumble after desire until remorse splits your liver
   like an arrow.[67]

7:24–25

Is there no defense against desire?
Listen to me, and heed the words of my mouth:
Let wisdom reign in your heart,[68]
and do not race after every emotion.
Do not assume that pleasure is the same as goodness
or that feelings are a guide to righteousness.
Desire has slain many mightier than you.
The way of undisciplined desire leads only to the grave,
the chambers of death are full of those who lacked the
   strength.

69 Wisdom is not passive. She does not withdraw from the world and wait for you to find her. On the contrary, she is in the world calling to you at every step. You don't have to find Wisdom; you only have to realize she has found you.

70 Wisdom does not reserve herself for the saint or the sage. She is just as eager to embrace the simple and the weak. Nor does she ask of you more than you can do. If you are not ready to become wise, at least let her keep you from being foolish.

71 Who is the "one who understands"? Not everyone is ready for Wisdom. Some, as she has told us a moment ago, are only ready to avoid foolishness and evil. Yet there are those, few or many, who are seeking simple truths free from convolution. These are those ready to understand. This may be you today. If you heed the way of Wisdom, it will be you tomorrow.

The Eighth Teaching

8:1–5

Do not think that Wisdom is silent in the face of desire.
She calls out boldly, her voice rising above the din.
There is nowhere she fears to go.[69]
Atop distant mountains,
on crowded highways,
at the crossroads of decision
she stands ready to guide you.
By the city gates,
even at the doorway of destruction she cries out to you:
Listen to me!
If you are too simple to discern wisdom,
at least let me teach you how to avoid evil.
If you are wise enough to know better and
yet weak enough to succumb to desire,
at least let me show you how to use your discretion,
to exercise control over random passions.[70]

8:6–9

Wisdom says:
Listen, for I will speak noble thoughts;
my mouth will utter honest words.
I will speak only truth to you,
for wickedness is poison to my lips.
I will speak of righteousness without twisted logic or perverted reasons.
One who understands will recognize the purity of my words
and the integrity of my teaching.[71]

(continued on page 53)

72 The value of the way of Wisdom cannot be measured in money. The wealth valued by society is not the wealth valued by Wisdom. She values honesty, simplicity, compassion, and justice. Society pays lip service to these values but places them lower than its preferred values: power and profit.

73 The words of Wisdom are spoken with no reference to God. Indeed, she says of herself things most often reserved for God.

74 Compassion is for you to choose, and when you do, justice will follow. Justice is secondary to compassion, because compassion is rooted in the unity and interdependence of self and others. You cannot love your neighbor as yourself without realizing that your neighbor is yourself. Once this realization is grasped, justice—treating others with the same respect and dignity with which you wish to be treated— is axiomatic.

8:10–11

Choose inner discipline over silver,
and knowledge over the finest gold.
My way is superior to pearls
and is of more value than anything else.[72]

8:12–17

I am Wisdom;
I dwell in watchfulness;
I provide insight into the way of life.
The godly reject evil.
I reject even the paths to evil:
the paths of pride, arrogance, and a lying tongue.
My words are counsel and guide;
I am understanding, and in me is strength.
Through me flows all justice and righteousness;
from me comes discernment and leadership.
I love those who love me
and reveal myself fully to those who search me out.[73]

8:18–20

Integrity and honor are my wealth,
and great good fortune lies with me.
My fruit is more precious than the finest gold;
it is superior to the choicest silver.
If you take up the path of compassion,
I will lead you along the road of justice.[74]

(continued on page 55)

75 Wisdom is the way things are. She is the grain in jade, the current of the oceans and the winds. To know her is to know the way of all things, for she is the means by which all things were created.

76 Here is one of the rare references to God in the Book of Proverbs. God and Wisdom are not equal, the One coming before the other. Wisdom is the first expression of God, the primal emanation of godliness. Wisdom comes from God, and creation comes from Wisdom.

77 The nature of Wisdom is joy and delight. This is how you can tell if one is wise: he takes joy and delight in life, and brings joy and delight to the living.

8:21–31

I fill the hearts of those who love me,
they will never lack for insight.
I am the deep grain of creation, the subtle current of life.[75]
God fashioned me before all things;[76]
I am the blueprint of creation.
I was there from the beginning, from before there was a beginning.
I am independent of time and space, earth and sky.
I was before depth was conceived,
before springs bubbled with water,
before the shaping of mountains and hills,
before God fashioned the earth and its bounty,
before the first dust settled on the land.
When God prepared the heavens, I was there.
When the circle of the earth was etched into the face of the deep, I was there.
When the stars and planets soared into their orbit,
when the deepest oceans found their level
and the dry land established the shores,
I was there.
I stood beside God as firstborn and friend.
My nature is joy, and I gave God constant delight.
Now that the world is inhabited, I rejoice in it.
I will be your true delight if you will heed my teachings.[77]

(continued on page 57)

78 Joy, happiness, liveliness, and grace are the signs of Wisdom and the wise. Cynicism and a jaundiced personality are the signs of the foolish.

8:32–36

So listen to me:
Follow me and be happy.
Practice my discipline and grow wise.
Abandon cynicism and jaded thought.
I bring joy to those who listen;
I bring happiness to those who attend me.
Like watchmen at their post they do not stray.
They see the play of wisdom.
Find me and find life.
Find me and find grace.
Turn your back on me and choose death.[78]

79 Wisdom is firm and cannot be shaken by the storms of doubt and despair. While there will be times of depression, these cannot overturn the Wisdom resting in your heart.

80 Like the later rabbis, including Jesus, Wisdom teaches through table fellowship. She invites us to sit and dine with her. In the company of other seekers, filled with fine food, we are more apt to open ourselves to her teaching. Some will come simply because she calls. Others need to be enticed with the promise of a meal. But she makes no distinction and favors no one over the other. She welcomes us as we come to her. If you are to practice the way of Wisdom, you too must learn the way of table fellowship, inviting strangers to dine with you and filling them with food both material and spiritual.

81 Struggling to defeat selfish desires only puts the self at the center of your attention. Do not waste time and energy defeating desire; turn instead to Wisdom and let desire crumble of its own accord.

The Ninth Teaching

9:1–6
Wisdom's house rests on many pillars.[79]
It is magnificent and easy to find.
Inside, she has cooked a fine meal and sweetened her wine
    with water.
Her table is set.
She sends maidens to the tallest towers to summon you.
To the simple they call:
Come, enter here.
To those who lack understanding they say:
Come, eat my food, drink my wine.
Abandon your empty life, and walk in the way of understanding.[80]

9:7–9
Wrestling with desire
fans its embers into flame.
Besides, your arguments are met with scorn,
and your energy could be put to better use.
Rebuking desire makes it the center of attention.
Turn your attention to Wisdom and let desire cool from
    neglect.
Wisdom thrives on discipline; truth flourishes when error is
    corrected.[81]

(continued on page 61)

82 Wonder is a state of selfless awe. In moments of wonder, your sense of separate self dissolves, and there is simply a timeless sense of ineffable bliss. Wisdom brings you to this state of wonder. Indeed, wonder is the foundation of Wisdom.

83 The wise act without having to choose right from wrong. Knowing one cup contains fresh water and another a fatal poison, do you actually choose between them? No, you drink the water and feel no compulsion to drink the poison. When you are filled with wisdom, what is true of water is true of good, and what is true of poison is true of evil. The wise do what is good not by choice but by the fact that they are wise.

84 Those who scorn the way of Wisdom, even if they do not actively pursue the way of foolishness, find themselves forever struggling between this and that, good and evil, right and wrong. Nothing is clear, and as often as not they choose that which poisons their lives. They do this not out of malice but out of ignorance. Wisdom does not combat malice. Wisdom replaces ignorance, and without ignorance, malice dissolves by itself.

85 It would be nice if Wisdom's voice were the only voice calling to you. Sadly, this isn't the case. Lady Wisdom has her opposite, Lady Folly. She too has her house, though it is not secured by pillars. And she too has her maids who seek to entice you. How can you tell the one from the other? So sure is Folly of your lack of discernment that she tells you her water is stolen and her bread is to be eaten in secret. There is nothing stolen and nothing hidden in Wisdom, but Folly demands theft and secrets. If the way offered you demands theft and you are forbidden to share what it is you are taught, you can be certain you have dined with Folly.

9:10–12

Those who walk with Wisdom walk in wonder.[82]

Marvel at the miracle of life, and gain understanding.

Stand in awe of the mystery, and enter the eternal present.

Become wise and you understand who you are:

you know what moves you, and you act almost without
effort.[83]

If you scorn this path, your heart is diminished,

your mind clouded, and you carry a heavy burden.

Everything you do goes awry.[84]

9:13–18

Wisdom is not the only voice you will hear.

Foolishness too has her house and her servants.

She sits at the doorway of her house and flaunts ignorance as
if it were gold.

Her servants also climb the city's towers and call out to you:

To the simple they say: *Turn in here.*

To those whose hearts are dry they say:

You think Wisdom's wine is sweet?

My stolen water is even sweeter.

You think Wisdom's feast is filling?

Eat my bread in secret and your mouth will taste true pleasure.

Do you know she sleeps with corpses?

Do you know her house is the gateway to the grave?[85]

1 The original Hebrew speaks of the joy of one's father and the sorrow of one's mother, but the implication is far greater. Heaven is the higher, more inclusive level of consciousness that realizes the interdependence of all in All. Earth is where your wisdom or lack thereof, your awareness or ignorance of unity plays itself out. To bring joy to the father is to bring joy to the mother as well, but if you lack the knowledge of life's interdependence and the moral obligation to engage life with compassion, you will only wreak havoc wherever you go.

2 You cannot escape dying; what matters is how you live. If you live miserly, your name quickly fades after death. If you used your life to invest in the lives of others, their lives are your immortality.

3 Wisdom is the realization of your union with life and the Source of Life. No matter how little you have in hand, your heart is full, and that fullness feeds the belly. Sin tears at the fabric of unity, creating a false but convincing illusion of alienation that starves you of peace and love by stuffing you with anxiety and fear.

4 The softest whisper is the awareness of God as the Source and Substance of all reality hovering just beneath your conscious mind. This awareness is the constant companion of the wise. The loudest alarm is the growing fear that gnaws at the ignorant, robbing them of any true tranquility.

☐ The First Collection of Shorter Sayings

10:1

These are the proverbs of Solomon:
Be wise and increase the joy of heaven;
Be foolish and increase the suffering of earth.[1]

10:2

Death cannot be bribed,
but generosity outlasts the grave.[2]

10:3

In famine, wisdom fills the belly,
while sin brings starvation even in the midst of plenty.[3]

10:4

Tip the balance by lying and your life is impoverished;
uphold honesty and the result is prosperity.

10:5

The wise learn from the softest whisper;
the ignorant sleep through the loudest alarm.[4]

5 You are whom you hang with. If you befriend the wise, wisdom will grow within you. If you befriend the wicked, their wickedness will seem the norm and you will do as they do.

6 Innocence—living without deceit—cannot protect you from the suffering that is natural to life: accident, illness, old age, and death. But it will prevent you from the self-inflicted horrors that arise when you live a lie.

7 When you fail to see the reality of God in, with, and as all things, you are sad, imagining and living with the illusion of alienation. But when you pretend to know what you do not, you are forced to protect a lie that even the slightest breeze can tear.

8 Anger arises when you imagine another to be thwarting your dreams. Love reveals that the other is simply trapped in his or her own quest for happiness. Anger fuels the illusory; love sees through it.

10:6
The good reap blessings;
the wicked chew on violence.

10:7
Seek out the righteous and blessings will follow;
yearning for the wicked brings ruin.[5]

10:8
The wise heart listens to others;
a foolish tongue wears out its audience.

10:9
Walk in innocence and you are safe from harm;
walk in deceit and your every step is revealed.[6]

10:10
Inner confusion leads to sadness;
laying false claim to wisdom makes you anxious.[7]

10:11
Straight talk is a wellspring of life;
deception is a mask for violence.

10:12
Anger sharpens every conflict;
but love enables suffering to pass quickly.[8]

10:13
Innocent mistakes are soon corrected;
deliberate evil invites a blow on the back.

9 Life is complex, but not complicated. The wise live simply, their hearts rooted in love, their eyes open to the interdependence of all things. The foolish live anxiously, their hearts rooted in greed, their eyes closed to all but their own desires. The wise need rarely to explain; the foolish exhaust themselves in excuses.

10 The wise rarely get angry, and when they do it is anger at the injustices of society rather than anger over their own thwarted dreams. This is because they know that there is no plan for one's life, only the challenges of living whatever life presents with grace, humor, courage, creativity, and compassion. The foolish, however, project their likes and dislikes onto God and imagine that success is their due rather than the result of their doing. Because the wise expect only what is, their anger is rare. Because the foolish expect only what they desire, their anger and frustration are constant.

11 Words can hurt as well as heal, and like a good medicine, healing words must be prepared thoughtfully and in advance. Babbling is the fools' futile attempt to fill the emptiness of their lives, and in their rush to speak their words are more often poison than balm.

10:14
The words of the wise are few;
the babbling of fools leads to ruin.⁹

10:15
Wisdom protects wealth;
ignorance induces only poverty.

10:16
Wise deeds bring life;
wickedness hastens death.

10:17
The disciplined live;
the lazy are lost.

10:18
No words, however pleasant, conceal the seething of an
    angry heart;
and one who gives voice to every hurt is a fool.¹⁰

10:19
The more you talk, the more you risk offense;
the wise purse their lips in silence.¹¹

12 What shrivels the heart is the illusion of alienation, the sense that you live in a zero-sum world where in order for you to win, others must lose. Endless competition rather than wise cooperation dries up the heart with anger and worry.

13 The wise know all things come to all people and hence fear nothing. The foolish imagine they can avoid what they fear and inadvertently make it the focus of their lives.

14 Because the wicked and the foolish seek to control life rather than encounter it, they fall victim to the very things they fear and seek to avoid. The wise surrender the illusion of control and simply respond to reality as it is. The wisdom of surrender and response is the key to living well.

15 Living in a state of wonder leaves you curious about what is and what is to come. Life is an unfolding experiment, and each moment a surprise to be met. This way of living is expansive. The foolish live anxious lives, worrying that the next moment will bring what they fear. Living anxiously robs them of wonder, and they seek to make each moment a replica of the last; there is no unfolding, and hence their lives seem short and dull.

10:20
The words of the wise are precious;
the heart of the wicked is shriveled.[12]

10:21
Wise words nourish many;
but the ignorant starve for lack of understanding.

10:22
Wisdom alone brings riches;
worrying never improves a situation.

10:23
Evil is the pastime of the foolish;
wisdom the play of the wise.

10:24
What you fear, you will find;
the wise desire only wisdom.[13]

10:25
Wickedness is devastated by the storm,
but wisdom is the foundation of the world.[14]

10:26
Just as vinegar sets your teeth on edge
and smoke stings your eyes,
half-hearted effort is doomed to failure.

10:27
Wonder enhances life;
worry shortens it.[15]

16 We stumble when we do not see what is in front of us. The right-eous live with eyes wide open, the light of Wisdom illuminating the ground before them. Still, the surrounding darkness is great, and even the wise may take a wrong turn. The wicked lack light. Not only will they, like the righteous, take wrong turns, but they will also trip over every obstacle along the way.

17 Don't imagine some future reward and punishment. Know that each moment is complete in itself. Doing good expands the heart then and there; doing evil contracts it.

18 The wealth of the wicked is rooted in selfishness. Selfishness is rooted in excessive concern for self. Excessive concern with self makes you angry. Hence, wealth cannot pacify anger but is in fact consumed by it. The just are rooted in community, knowing self and other to be part of a greater unity. Their generosity lessens the self and frees them from selfishness and the anger that accompanies it.

10:28
The righteous anticipate only gladness;
the hope of the wicked is tainted by fear.

10:29
The path of God strengthens the innocent;
those who build with iniquity raise only ruins.

10:30
The righteous never stumble;
the wicked are never tranquil.[16]

10:31
The words of the wise ripen on the vine;
the yapping of fools shrivels on the ground.

11:1
Blessed are those whose judgment is honest
and whose scales are balanced,
but the deceitful pervert the way of God.

11:2
Arrogance is its own disgrace;
modesty its own reward.[17]

11:3
The just are guided by simplicity;
the wicked seed corruption with complication.

11:4
No matter how wealthy the wicked, anger destroys them;
The generosity of the just saves them from danger.[18]

19 All things come to all people. Do not imagine the wicked alone encounter evil or that the wise are never tempted. The difference between them is not the life they meet, but the values they nourish. The wicked cherish evil and draw it to them. The wise shun it and seek only the good.

11:5

Justice smoothes a pitted path,
but the wicked stumble over their own evil.

11:6

The wise are rescued by justice,
but the wicked are trapped by their own lies.

11:7

When the wicked die, their schemes die with them,
and the hope of their accomplishments is shattered.

11:8

There is evil in this world, and the wicked attract it like a
    magnet;
the just are wise enough to not be ensnared.[19]

11:9

The wicked speak in order to harm;
the wise use words to heal.

11:10

People rejoice when the good are rewarded;
they also rejoice at the misfortune of the wicked.

11:11

The prosperity of the just is shared by the community,
but the wicked sow discord and rob the people of blessing.

11:12

The empty-hearted are quick to criticize;
a heart filled with understanding values silence.

20 Just as the wise are not immune to meeting evil without, neither are they immune to encountering it within. The wise and the wicked are both human, and all humans share passions both just and unjust. What moves the wicked to evil and the wise to justice is not only their inner preferences and values, but also the inner preferences and values of those with whom they congregate. When living with the wicked, evil seems good. When living with the wise, justice seems good. Bind yourself to the wise and you will be called to goodness.

21 Greed is an attitude for which there is no satisfaction. Whatever you have, you feel compelled to have more. You stuff yourself with goods as if that were a good in and of itself. But since there is no satisfaction, you continue to consume until you choke. The generous find satisfaction in each act of giving. They may acquire goods, but the good is in sharing what they have and not simply in having it. The greedy are never happy, for greed is never finished. The generous are never unhappy, for there is always something to share.

22 A selfish heart is a heart closed in upon itself and lives trapped in the illusion of self and other. Imprisoned in the illusion of isolated self, the selfish cannot know God, for God is the One that shatters the illusion of self and the plague of selfishness. Where the selfish see the other, the open-hearted see God.

11:13
The wicked are a font of gossip;
the faithful protect every confidence.

11:14
You cannot control your nature alone;
salvation lies in listening to the wise.[20]

11:15
The wicked default on their loans,
but the wise honor their commitments.

11:16
Honor is retained through graciousness;
power is maintained through intimidation.

11:17
The kind attract kindness from others;
the cruel are a plague upon themselves.

11:18
The wicked choke on their greed,
but the generous find happiness in the act of giving.[21]

11:19
The selfless inherit life,
but the reward of the self-centered is death.

11:20
A selfish heart cannot find God;
an open heart cannot lose God.[22]

23 The generous live with open hands, giving when they have something to give, and receiving when they need to receive. The stingy live with closed fists, clinging to what they have and incapable of opening to more when they have nothing at all.

24 The foolish imagine they are self-sufficient; the wise know they must be self-reliant. Being self-sufficient leaves you with the lie that you do not need others; being self-reliant opens you to the truth that while you must do what you can, you cannot do all you need done. Knowing your limitations allows you to reach out to others for help. Knowing their limitations allows you to reach out to others to help.

11:21

Evil influence reaches no farther than the wicked's arm,
but good deeds are a raft for generations.

11:22

A golden ring cannot hide a pig's snout,
nor a beautiful face disguise an evil heart.

11:23

The righteous trust in goodness;
the wicked place their hope in anger.

11:24

The generous are not anxious about wealth;
the stingy always fear poverty.[23]

11:25

Share in another's joy and your own joy is kindled;
fill the bellies of the hungry and your own stomach is filled.

11:26

One who hoards is cursed;
one who shares is blessed.

11:27

Seek the happiness of others and you will find God;
seek their destruction and you will fall into your own snare.

11:28

Trust in your own power and fail;
know your limitations and flourish.[24]

25 Being of two minds means being split between likes and dislikes. One mind is then pitted against the other in a mad and futile effort to cling to what you like and keep what you don't like at bay. The truth is otherwise: life includes joy and suffering, likes and dislikes. The wise learn to accept what is and move on. The foolish seek to control what is and remain stuck in their illusion. Live among the wise and you will learn to prosper from reality. Live among the foolish and you will reap only frustration.

26 Doing good begets good—this is the path of the righteous. But the wise go one step farther. Knowing that the lost are not evil in themselves, but only trapped in evil because they have failed to see through the illusion of self, selfishness, and the zero-sum world self and selfishness imagine, the wise seek to bring wisdom to the lost and show them the truth that is the inheritance of all.

27 The truth of reality is reality itself: the good and the bad, the desired and the undesired. The wise see what is and engage it creatively with compassion and justice. The wicked are filled with anxiety, fear, and anger and see these reflected back to them in all the world. They live in their own reflection and are consumed by their own fears.

28 The way of the wise is not easy, and securing knowledge is itself a discipline. Do not imagine the wise become wise without effort or that living wisely is effortless as well. Rather, the wise constantly discipline themselves to reality, knowing what is and conforming to it. The wise work with the grain of life, avoiding the excessive effort demanded by working against it, but this is not to say that effort itself is not necessary.

29 Part of the discipline of the wise is listening to the pain of those you may have injured. Do not imagine that being wise, you will cause others no suffering. Know that even the wise make mistakes, but unlike the foolish, they learn from them.

11:29
Be of two minds and your legacy is the wind;
bond with the wise and enjoy prosperity.[25]

11:30
Righteousness sows the seeds of life;
Wisdom redeems the souls of the lost.[26]

11:31
The wise see truth all around them;
the wicked are rewarded with their own malice.[27]

12:1
Love knowledge and you will value discipline;[28]
only the stupid are deaf to criticism.[29]

12:2
A good person is a conduit for the truth,
and a schemer a sluice for evil.

12:3
Wickedness is built on a weak foundation,
but righteousness can withstand any disaster.

12:4
A faithful spouse can save a faltering marriage,
but an unfaithful one hastens its demise.

12:5
The mind of the wise is uncluttered and open;
the mind of the wicked is crowded with schemes.

30 The hurt caused by the wise is never deliberate, while that caused by the wicked always is. The wise can err, and when they do, others may be hurt. But knowing this, the wise are vigilant to the suffering they cause and are quick to make amends. The wicked justify all their deeds by their endless quest for self-satisfaction. Valuing self over other, they see the suffering they cause merely as collateral damage in their quest for the greater good: their own happiness.

31 Again, we must distinguish between self-reliance and self-sufficiency. The wise are self-reliant, doing what they can for themselves (and others), and reaching out to others when their limits are reached. The foolish, here called the pompous, are obsessed with self-sufficiency: they believe they are complete unto themselves and that others are to serve them. The wise create a world of sharing; the wicked, a world of hoarding. In the world of the wise, all are fed. In the world of the wicked, even they will come to starvation.

12:6
Even the pleasant words of the wicked intend violence,
while the misstatements of the wise come from a loving
    heart.[30]

12:7
The wicked die and leave a legacy of wind;
the righteous die and leave a legacy of life.

12:8
Wisdom draws praise,
a twisted heart only shame.

12:9
The simple are satisfied, serving themselves,
while the pompous starve waiting to be fed.[31]

12:10
The humane care for their animals,
the thoughtless neglect them.

12:11
Till the soil of your character and reap goodness;
the pursuit of pleasure leads the heart astray.

12:12
The wicked are driven by jealousy; in the end they have
    nothing.
The root of the wise is grounded in integrity.

32 When you live from truth, as best as it can be known, there is no need to lie. The fabric of your life is truth. When you live from lies, the fabric of truth is replaced by the fabrication of lies. Living a fiction, you cannot remember the truth and worry that your secrets may be revealed.

33 The foolish live a life that demands justification. So filled with error and pain, they have to make excuses for their mistakes. The wise know they will err and seek not to justify it but to correct it. To see where they err, the wise seek the guidance of the just. The foolish argue in favor of their foolishness; the wise look to those wiser still to show them where they need to grow.

34 The wise know that thoughts and feelings arise of their own accord and are beyond conscious control. We only know what we are thinking after we have already thought it; we only know what we are feeling after we have felt it. The wise seek not to control but to observe; they watch the wildness of thoughts and feelings without judgment and act justly regardless of what they are thinking and feeling. The foolish imagine they can control their thoughts and feelings and become frustrated when they fail to do so. Worse still, they allow thoughts and feelings to determine their actions, often leading to behavior as wild and as uncontrollable as the thoughts and feelings themselves.

12:13
Guard your tongue and have no fear;
honesty frees you from worry.[32]

12:14
Right speech is wise speech;
right action brings its own reward.

12:15
The foolish justify their folly;
the wise seek the counsel of the just.[33]

12:16
The ignorant react with anger;
the wise watch their emotions come and go.[34]

12:17
Make truth a habit and your words will be trusted;
bear false witness and you become the epitome of deceit.

12:18
The tongue of the wicked cuts like a sharp sword;
the words of the wise bring healing.

12:19
Truth is forever;
falsehood lasts but a moment.

12:20
Plot evil and your heart drowns in deceit;
counsel peace and you are filled with joy.

35 The ultimate truth cannot be spoken, for it lies outside the limits of language. Knowing this, the wise speak little, using their words to point beyond words. The foolish imagine that they can create the truth for themselves, and use words—often deceitful words—to do so. It is not difficult to differentiate the wise from the foolish: the more words a person uses to articulate that which is beyond words, the more foolish that person is.

12:21
Act justly and do not worry about consequences;
act wickedly and fear every turn.

12:22
Dishonesty exiles you from God;
speak truth and God will seek you out.

12:23
The wise value silence;
the ignorant prefer to babble.[35]

12:24
Diligence is its own reward;
the dreams of the lazy die at dawn.

12:25
Do not give in to worry;
do good and overwhelm worry with joy.

12:26
The wise overlook the foibles of others;
the wicked obsess about them.

12:27
Success through guile will not last;
wealth gained honestly endures forever.

12:28
Generosity is the way to life;
even death cannot block its path.

36 The wise know that wisdom is rooted in experience; hence, they value those who have used their experience to become wise. The foolish imagine that they alone can fathom the truth; the experience of their elders is only an annoyance. And yet, do not imagine that experience equals wisdom. The foolish do not lack for experience; they lack for understanding. Living in the isolated and alienating world of self-sufficiency, their experience is a mirror into themselves. They learn nothing new because they see nothing new. Experience yields wisdom only when used to free yourself from self-sufficiency and place yourself in the position of giving and receiving to all you meet.

37 The path is the ground beneath your feet, the events that happen to you moment to moment. The way is both your destination and the quality of your walking: walking justly and compassionately regardless of where the path takes you. Sometimes the connection between the two is clear, sometimes it is murky. Sometimes the path seems to lead you closer to your goal, sometimes farther from it. If you focus on the path, you can feel lost and fearful, and give in to anger and blame. If you focus on the way, keeping your final destination in mind, and taking care to walk each step in peace, you are never lost, no matter how wide a detour the path takes. The wise keep their eyes on the way; the foolish stare only at the path.

38 It is good to be generous, to share what you have with those who have less. It is better to do so with the proper realization: you are not giving what is yours to someone else; you are sharing with someone else that which belongs to you both. The foolish share and think they are made less by the act of sharing, losing their possessions in hopes of accruing merit. But the wise share and know there is no making less or more, only a more just distribution of what belongs to us all.

13:1
The wise child welcomes the advice of elders;
the foolish ignores anything they suggest.[36]

13:2
The wise are nourished by the fruit of their words,
but the wicked choke on violence.

13:3
Guard your tongue and you guard your soul;
speak without reflection and you invite disaster.

13:4
Lust drains the soul;
honest labor fills it to the brim.

13:5
The wise despise falsehood;
the wicked traffic therein.

13:6
Observe the truth and the way is clear;
ignore it and you lose direction.[37]

13:7
Pretending to knowledge reveals your lack of it;
admitting ignorance is the beginning of genius.

13:8
Merit may be gained by generosity,
but generosity without compassion is worth nothing.[38]

39 The difference between the good and the wicked is not that one is a lamp and the other isn't, but that both are lamps but only one is lighted. The wicked are not lost to wickedness, only lost to darkness. If they draw close enough to the wise, the fire of Wisdom will ignite the yet unlit lamp and both will glow with joy, and wickedness will cease.

40 This and the prior verse go together: wisdom requires concentration; foolishness is the hallmark of distraction. The discipline of Wisdom teaches you how to focus your attention, how to concentrate your mind that you might see through the surface of things into the unified center. Those who do so can see the consequences of their actions and are thus apt to act more wisely. Those who cannot do so act in the moment and are surprised and often troubled by the next.

13:9
The good are aflame with joy;
the lamp of the wicked is not yet lit.[39]

13:10
A closed mind causes strife;
an open mind cultivates wisdom.

13:11
Easy money vanishes fast;
honest effort adds value to every success.

13:12
Breaking a promise causes heartache;
keeping a promise is a Tree of Life.

13:13
Belittling the truth invites trouble;
honoring the truth is its own reward.

13:14
The sage's teaching is a well of life;
its waters can save you from an early death.

13:15
An attentive mind flourishes;
a distracted mind is barren.

13:16
Be wise and reflect before you act;
a fool follows every whim heedlessly.[40]

41 This verse and the prior verse go together: the wise learn to act only when appropriate and thus free themselves from their passions without having to control the passions themselves. Free from passion means you are capable of witnessing the thoughts and feelings that arise in you without the need to act on them. The fool may seek the same freedom but pursues it through the false notion that thoughts and feelings can be controlled by the will, when in fact only actions can be controlled.

42 When a wise person dies, her mistakes are forgotten in the telling and retelling of her wisdom and generosity. When a foolish person dies, her good deeds are forgotten in the telling and retelling of her wickedness.

43 There are two kinds of justice: retributive and distributive. The first focuses on punishment, the second on fairness. The wicked seek to punish those who fail to live up to their standard; the wise seek a standard that allows everyone the opportunity to flourish.

13:17
One who is faithless will be betrayed;
one who is trustworthy invites the support of others.

13:18
One who lacks self-control is despised;
one who learns to curb desire is respected.

13:19
Detachment from desire frees the soul,
but the fool is a slave to every passion.[41]

13:20
Walk with the wise and gain wisdom;
keep company with fools and you will regret it.

13:21
The evil are pursued by evil;
the good are rewarded with good.

13:22
The legacy of the wise is eternal;
the wicked leave nothing, even their merit is buried with
    them.[42]

13:23
The poor can labor hard and bring in the harvest,
but without justice they will reap no benefit.[43]

13:24
Undisciplined parents produce unruly children;
good parents provide counsel and guidance.

44 A home is sustained with love. Wisdom cultivates love by revealing the interdependence of each family member. When you know the other as yourself, you will love the other as yourself. Even in a family, the foolish live in self-isolation, competing with those they seek to love rather than cooperating with them. The foolish imagine that for one to win, others must lose. The wise know differently: no one wins unless everyone wins.

45 Or so it appears. God is everywhere and everything, so there is no "alone." But the wicked see themselves cut off from everyone and everything and hence refuse to see the One who is with them and in them at every moment.

13:25
The wise are satisfied with whatever they eat;
the wicked remain hungry no matter how much they
consume.

14:1
Wisdom sustains the home;
foolishness destroys it.[44]

14:2
God is with those whose paths are straight;
those whose paths are dishonest walk alone.[45]

14:3
The arrogant choke on their own scorn;
the wise learn to restrain the tongue.

14:4
Without oxen, the trough is clean, but there is no harvest;
without discipline, life seems easy, but there is no wisdom.

14:5
Train yourself in honesty
and your word will be trusted.

14:6
Liars are not believed even when they speak the truth;
but those with integrity find discrimination easy.

14:7
Take nothing seriously
and your lips will never know wisdom.

46 Knowing yourself is the beginning of wisdom. Look deeply into yourself and you discover "you" is not an isolated being, but a flowering of that infinite system of *be-ing* we call God. The foolish never grasp the truth of who they are and cannot engage others except from the perspective of falsehood.

47 If bitterness itself can be made sweet, then nothing is fixed. The unfixed nature of life, the flow of everything into its opposite over and over, is the hidden meaning of this proverb. Nothing is kept from either the wise or the foolish; both will know bitterness, and both will know sweetness. The difference between them is that the wise do not cling to bitterness and let it become sweet over time, while the foolish never let it go, insisting that another can transform it for them.

48 The foolish are always in a hurry. They imagine there is a reward awaiting them just around the corner and race to find it. The wise never hurry; they know the reward is this moment only. The foolish rush to escape suffering and embrace joy, and race even through joy, hoping for yet a greater joy up ahead. The wise cling to nothing and race after nothing, but drink deep of whatever is present at the moment. In this way they suffer no longer than is necessary and never miss an opportunity for joy.

14:8
True wisdom is self-understanding;
it is themselves who fools really deceive.[46]

14:9
Foolish desires taste of guilt;
just desires are sweet on the tongue.

14:10
Only you know the bitterness in your heart,
and no stranger can sweeten it for you.[47]

14:11
A strong fortress will fall if built on deceit;
a flimsy tent will hold if pitched on justice.

14:12
The shortest route is not always the best;
sometimes it leads to death.[48]

14:13
Even good-natured teasing may cause distress;
be sure that laughter does not end in tears.

14:14
A heart filled with pride has lost its way;
the good learn to rise above it.

14:15
The ignorant believe every rationalization;
the wise consider every word.

49 Feelings justify nothing. They are complete in themselves. If you are angry, feel angry, but do not use your feelings to justify angry and hurtful deeds.

50 Expressing every feeling that passes into your awareness enslaves you with a wild mind. Simply observe your feelings and only act on those that promote compassion and justice. But what is true of feelings is not true of deeds. While it is wise to wait and observe your feelings before taking action, once the right action is known, doing is demanded. Holding back on deeds that must be done is foolish.

51 Life isn't just. The wicked do prosper and the righteous do suffer. The wise are not dismayed by this. They know that all things come to all people and place their trust not in the short-term success of the wicked, but in the long-term goodness of the wise.

52 Lest you imagine that foolishness is a matter of class, this and the prior proverb speak to foolishness of the poor. They too are enamored with the rich, hoping to catch the crumbs that might fall from their tables. But it isn't wealth that truly matters, but generosity. Let the rich who are wise give generously, and let the poor who are wise do no less.

14:16
The wise recognize their anger and hold it in check;
the ignorant use anger to justify their actions.[49]

14:17
A short temper enslaves you;
those who procrastinate are disliked.[50]

14:18
Fools inherit folly;
the wealth of the wise is knowledge.

14:19
The wicked may prosper, yet the wise do not envy them;
wisdom always rules over wealth.[51]

14:20
Even the poor ignore the poor,
but everyone seeks the company of the rich.

14:21
Those who neglect the poor betray the community;
only the generous are praiseworthy.[52]

14:22
Sow evil and reap evil;
sow good and harvest mercy and truth.

14:23
Effort brings you joy;
idleness brings you sorrow.

53 Fear of God is rooted in the notion that you are other than God. Faith in God reveals that God is manifesting as you. Fear of God leads to fear of others, especially those whose God may be different from your own. Faith in God leads to love of others, regardless of the Name they give to the Nameless. Fear of God may keep you from doing what is wrong, but faith in God will empower you to do what is right. In this your loved ones are protected.

54 Everyone dies. But those who die with faith die into the greater Unity from which they came and in which they live. Those who die with fear see themselves as separate and their death as making the separation permanent.

14:24
The crown of the wise is their integrity;
the ignorant always dress in foolishness.

14:25
Truth saves lives;
self-deception destroys them.

14:26
Fear of God may keep you from error,
but faith in God protects not only you but those you love.[53]

14:27
Faith is the source of life,
diverting you from the snares of death.[54]

14:28
The authority of kings comes from the people;
they have no power without a nation.

14:29
Patience is the sign of understanding;
a quick temper is the hallmark of fools.

14:30
A calm mind refreshes the body,
but jealousy disturbs you to your core.

14:31
Robbing from the poor is an insult to God;
caring for the poor honors God.

55 The wise have no need to display their wisdom. They are content simply to live with grace and humility, welcoming any who seek them out, but having no desire to advertise what they know. The foolish hawk their ignorance, hoping that a loud noise will distract people from the emptiness of the product being offered.

56 A nation that is torn by injustice, with the rich getting richer at the expense of the poor, is a nation soon crushed under the weight of its own need to oppress those with little so that the those with much can have yet more. A nation devoted to distributive justice, that sees to the needs of all, thrives. Yet generosity is more than simply flattening the distance between haves and have-nots. This indiscriminate kindness makes no differentiation between the wicked and the just or between the foolish and the wise. If all are rewarded the same, there is no opportunity for the wise and the just to rise and for the foolish and the wicked to fall.

57 Anger arises when our desires are thwarted. The wise desire little, so anger rarely haunts them. The mark of the foolish is a quick temper, for they are burdened with many lusts.

58 This is difficult for many of us to accept. We want a world that is free of evil, injustice, and suffering, but this isn't reality. The wise accept everything that befalls them, neither clinging to the good nor fleeing from the bad. They blame no one and simply turn their attention to what must be done. The foolish place themselves at the center of the universe, taking credit for the good, shifting responsibility for the bad, and devoting their energies to making sense of life rather than simply living it.

14:32
The wicked are brought down by their own evil,
but the wise are protected by their own integrity.

14:33
The wise heart is tranquil;
the foolish heart is ever on parade.[55]

14:34
Generosity can save a nation,
but indiscriminate kindness can be harmful.[56]

14:35
The wise serve others and are appreciated;
the self-absorbed are disdained.

15:1
A gentle response defuses anger;
harsh words incite more rage.[57]

15:2
The tongue of the wise imparts wisdom;
the mouth of the ignorant spreads folly.

15:3
You cannot escape from reality;
evil and good are visible to all.[58]

15:4
Gentle encouragement is a tree of life,
but critical words can murder the spirit.

59 Even the wise have their foibles. Thinking they have found the answer, they no longer entertain the questions that life continually poses. True wisdom isn't about finding answers; it is about sharpening questions.

60 Good and evil are like the positive and negative poles of a magnet. Neither can exist without the other, and yet there is no overcoming their opposition. The key isn't to do away with either pole or to erase the reality of opposites in some faux nonduality. Rather, the key is to realize that nonduality embraces duality, that the two and the one are part of a greater and ineffable whole.

61 We despair when we imagine that we are apart from, rather than a part of, the Greater Reality we call God. Just as a wave cannot be apart from the ocean, so we cannot be apart from God.

15:5
The arrogant reject all guidance;
the wise treasure it and become wiser.

15:6
The house of the wise is strong,
but complacency can ruin its foundation.[59]

15:7
The wise share their knowledge,
but angry hearts resent their efforts.

15:8
There is no reconciliation between good and evil;
therefore the wise pray for clarity.[60]

15:9
Dishonesty is a betrayal of your birthright;
through discrimination, freedom is found.

15:10
If you lack discipline, you reject good advice;
if you hate criticism, you are heading for disaster.

15:11
Never despair!
You heart is forever in God.[61]

15:12
The ignorant avoid the wise
and do not value their counsel.

62 The thorns that plague the lazy are the sharp challenges that life presents to everyone. Because the lazy prefer not to face them, they multiply and seem to block their path. The wise expect the thorns and trample them down, sometimes feeling their sting, but always moving on.

15:13
Happiness illumines the face in joy,
but a sad heart shrouds the spirit in despair.

15:14
A serious mind seeks understanding,
but a fool is satisfied with folly.

15:15
Those who envy are forever poor,
but the generous never lack for anything.

15:16
Better a little earned honestly,
than much won through deception.

15:17
Better a simple meal eaten with love,
than a feast eaten in bitterness.

15:18
Anger incites more anger;
patience leads to tranquility.

15:19
The lazy path is strewn with thorns;
the effortful road is smooth under foot.[62]

15:20
A wise child is a father's delight;
a stupid child is a mother's shame.

63 The foolish speak from scripts, seeking to insert their words into a situation regardless of what the situation may be. The wise have no script and speak only when they understand what is going on and if they believe their words can shed light upon it.

64 The ultimate folly is belief in permanence. Nothing lasts; everything dies. The fool denies this and grasps all the more tightly as life slips away. The wise live with open hands, allowing what needs to pass and remaining open to what is coming next.

65 The mansions of the arrogant are built on fear; the homes of the simple are built on love. While both will fade over time, love is the longer lasting.

15:21
The foolish heart is satisfied with folly;
the wise heart rejoices in justice.

15:22
Listen to no one and you will fail;
hear what others have to say and you will prosper.

15:23
An apt response is always welcome;
make sure your words fit the occasion.[63]

15:24
The wise walk with purpose,
untroubled by impermanence or death.[64]

15:25
The mansions of the arrogant will decay,
but the homes of the simple will outlast them.[65]

15:26
Evil thoughts pollute;
thoughtful words purify.

15:27
If wealth is ill-gotten,
even a palace is doomed.

15:28
Think before you speak;
the unrestrained tongue wreaks havoc.

66 There is no true separation from God, but you can convince your-self otherwise. The more you focus on self and give in to selfishness, the more isolated you feel and the more fearful you become. Isolation and fear feed the illusion of separateness. The wise know that God is all and that they, and you, are a part of the One and Only Reality. Knowing this, they focus on the whole rather than the part and act in harmony with it.

67 Wonder is a selfless state. At the moment of wonder, the finite self of ego is engulfed by the infinite grandeur of God and there is nothing but awe. When the moment passes and the self returns, it does so lighter than before, less defensive, more humble. The more awe you experience, the less awful you feel.

68 If God is the whole, and every part is an expression of it, then you are always speaking to God. Realizing every encounter is a God encounter, engage each moment with humility and respect.

15:29
Selfishness separates you from God;
selflessness awakens you to God.[66]

15:30
The truth gladdens the heart;
good news strengthens the bones.

15:31–32
Open your ears to guidance
and take your place among the wise.
Close your ears to counsel and you jeopardize your soul.
The wise heart welcomes truth.

15:33
The way to wisdom is through wonder;
the way to honor is through humility.[67]

16:1
Your mind may be full of confusion,
but always speak as if talking to God.[68]

16:2
Your mind can rationalize anything,
but your heart knows the truth.

16:3
Do whatever is kind
and the way will become clear.

69 Good and evil are like poles of a magnet. To be a magnet, both poles are required. Good and evil are the poles of God, reality, life as you live it. Do not imagine you can escape from either or that one is superior to the other. Although opposites, both are necessary. Knowing this, the wise learn to engage the dark as well as the light, cursing neither even as they seek to root themselves in the latter.

70 Aligned with godliness, you realize the nonduality of God. Realizing the nonduality of God, you know that both enemies and friends are divine. Knowing this, you treat both with respect and refuse to demonize the former. Without demonization, there is always the possibility of peace.

71 It isn't hard to become famous. It is hard to become famous for the right reason. Don't focus on fame and recognition. Know what is just and do it, and do not fret over self-advertisement.

72 You have lots of plans and dreams and may imagine a future in which all your desires are fulfilled. But if you pursue your dream at the expense of others, even if achieved it will be short-lived.

73 Do not obsess over thoughts and feelings. These rise and fall of their own accord. Focus on your actions: doing what is right, just, and good regardless of the drama playing out across your mind.

74 When arguing about good and evil, so many of us focus on the wickedness of extremes—Hitler, Stalin, Pol Pot—rather than on the everyday evil we excuse in the name of our own passions. Don't worry about evil until you have mastered the horrors you yourself commit.

16:4
Everything is from God;
even evil plays a role in the divine drama.[69]

16:5
Pride blinds you to the truth;
conceit corrupts every kindness.

16:6
If you turn from evil and stand in awe of God,
then your kindness and honesty will bring you forgiveness.

16:7
Align yourself with godliness
and even your enemies will make peace with you.[70]

16:8
Righteousness alone determines the value of your work;
fame without justice is hollow.[71]

16:9
Desire plots a course;
godliness secures the journey.[72]

16:10
Charming words cannot mask evil acts.
It is never the thought that counts, only the deed.[73]

16:11
Cosmic balance is in the hands of God;
you should worry only about your own integrity.[74]

75 | Many people can turn from evil and see the way of the good, but far fewer have the courage to walk it. The way of evil is the way of self taken to selfish extremes. The way of goodness is the way of the self leaning toward selflessness. Many who think they know better are too attached to selfishness to walk any other path.

16:12
Take no pleasure in evil;
security lies with truth alone.

16:13
Wise leaders desire truth,
and those who speak it are honored.

16:14
Anger has the power to destroy,
but the wise learn how to cool it.

16:15
The wise shed light on life;
their gifts are like rain falling on thirsty ground.

16:16
Seek wisdom over gold
and understanding more than silver.

16:17
Turn from evil and your road is paved smooth;
walk it and your soul is protected.[75]

16:18
Pride precedes a fall;
arrogance precedes a failure.

16:19
Better to be sad among the humble
than share the spoils of the proud.

76 The delusion is of a separate self and private victory. There is no success when success comes at the expense of others. All there is is mounting resentment. One who wins this way is forever afraid that those who lost will rise up and take what was won. There is no joy in such success, only growing fear.

77 If what you wish to say is false, there is no need to say it. But even if true, it may not be necessary. Speak only what is necessary and true, and find the most compassionate way to do so.

16:20
What secures success?
Wise investigation and aligning yourself with goodness.

16:21
A wise heart brings understanding;
sweetened speech attracts much learning.

16:22
The wise seek wisdom as the source of life;
the schemes of the ignorant are shrouded in delusion.[76]

16:23
A wise heart leads to right speech;
train your lips to speak the truth.[77]

16:24
Gentle words are like a honeycomb,
sweet to the soul and healing to the body.

16:25
Be aware of the consequences of your actions:
some things seem right at first glance,
but in the end they lead to destruction.

16:26
The quest for wisdom is its own reward;
let your actions be driven by truth.

16:27
The careless stir up slander as if it were a treasure,
their lips burn with envy's fire.

78 You cannot know the consequences of your actions, and even the most well-intentioned deed can bring sorrow. And yet you must act. Knowing you cannot know, act humbly. Knowing you cannot know, act justly. In this way, you can take comfort in having done what seemed right and thus engage the next moment without the baggage of the last.

16:28
A liar incites others to violence;
the grumbler alienates those who might be of help.

16:29
The violent arouse their friends
and lead them on the wrong path.

16:30
If your eyes are closed to truth, you will be deceived.
If your mouth is always open, you may say things you regret.

16:31
Those who are honorable
will find old age the crown of their achievements.

16:32
Patience is the greatest strength,
Self-control the key to success.

16:33
Do what is right, even without knowing the odds;
the outcome is known only by God.[78]

17:1
Eating a crust of bread in peace
is better than feasting in a strife-torn house.

17:2
An intelligent nanny will discipline a naughty child
and earn the love that is her due.

79 Refining pots and crucibles hold silver and gold and accomplish their work while doing so. The same is true of God. Your heart is held within the Divine, and it is there that it is purified.

80 Do not imagine your friends cannot hurt you. They can and over time most likely will. Knowing that we all are capable of hurting others should humble us and make us more forgiving of those who hurt us. If you wish to befriend only the perfect, you will have no friends at all.

17:3
A refining pot tries silver
and a crucible tries gold,
but only God can try the heart.[79]

17:4
No matter what is said, the troublemaker hears evil;
no matter how true it is, the liar believes it to be false.

17:5
Mock the poor and you insult the Creator;
rejoice at others' misfortune and you will suffer.

17:6
Grandchildren are a delight to old people;
parents are a joy to their children.

17:7
A liar who speaks the truth will not be believed;
falsehood is alien to those who are honest.

17:8
People who give bribes are deluded;
they imagine their success is secured.

17:9
Those who forgive insults keep their friends;
those who harp on faults are lonely.[80]

17:10
The wise learn something from every mistake;
the fool learns nothing from a hundred errors.

81 Wisdom does not secure wealth, nor does foolishness prohibit it. Even the greatest fool can get lucky now and then. What separates the wise from the foolish isn't their wealth but what they do with it. Both may hire teachers and guides, but only the wise are humble enough to consider their advice.

17:11
Those who seek profit through deceit
are cheated by those with whom they do business.

17:12
It is easier to deal with an angry bear
than a fool unconvinced of his foolishness.

17:13
If you repay good with evil,
evil will take root in your home.

17:14
Starting a quarrel is like opening a floodgate;
abandon the thought before you drown in anger.

17:15
Rationalizing evil and condemning good
both pervert the way of godliness.

17:16
Wealthy fools can afford teachers,
but they are too opinionated to heed them.[81]

17:17
A friend's love is always available,
but siblings are there in times of trouble.

17:18
Friendship may vanish
if you become business partners.

82 A twisted heart is one that is forever looking over its shoulder in fear. A twisted heart is one trapped in the zero-sum game of winners and losers, one that imagines everyone is out to steal what everyone else has. The only thing produced in such a world is paranoia.

83 The foolish imagine that God and truth are always at a distance and in the future. Theirs is a never-ending quest for the horizon. The wise know that God and truth are always here and now. Theirs is a never-ending quest to be present to the moment.

84 And yet we have to let our children make mistakes. The task of the parent is not to prevent our children from making mistakes, but to teach them how to learn from them when they do.

17:19
Betrayal breeds violence;
arrogance invites its own destruction.

17:20
A twisted heart cannot fathom goodness;
a lying tongue cannot speak truth.[82]

17:21
Encourage crime and fear haunts you;
allow others to be shamed and joy escapes you.

17:22
A glad heart is sure medicine;
despair, a cancer to the bone.

17:23
The wicked are quick to bribe
to divert the course of justice.

17:24
The wise find wisdom everywhere;
the ignorant look for it somewhere else.[83]

17:25
Parents fret over their children's mistakes;
it is a churning in their souls.[84]

17:26
The dishonest hate those who obey the law
and envy those who are generous to others.

85 This and the previous proverb go together. While silence is the hallmark of the wise, even the fool can learn to be quiet. Do not let yourself be deceived by outward tactics. Test not the silence of the wise or the foolish, but their words.

86 Falling prey to desires is not the same as having them. Desires, like all thoughts and feelings, arise into your conscious mind of their own accord. By the time you know you desire something, the desire has already risen and taken its place. Seeking to quell desires, like seeking to control thoughts and feelings, is a futile effort. By the time you know what you desire, think, and feel, you are already desiring, thinking, and feeling it. Falling prey means succumbing to a desire once it is known. Doing so puts you at the mercy of your subconscious from which desire arises. Instead, welcome whatever arises into your conscious mind, but entertain and act on only those desires, thoughts, and feelings that promote justice and compassion.

87 There are some spiritual philosophies that urge us to return kindness regardless of what we encounter. Yet this may allow evil to propagate. While it is never right to demonize another, it is right to recognize evil and respond to it properly. The proper response to evil is neither kindness nor evil, but justice.

17:27
Silence is a hallmark of wisdom;
the words of the wise are few.

17:28
Even fools can hold their tongues;
sealed lips do not always mean an understanding heart.[85]

18:1
Do not fall prey to desire,
for you will be disgraced among your peers.[86]

18:2
The ignorant express a desire for wisdom
only when their ignorance is exposed.

18:3
Contempt travels with evil;
insult accompanies disgrace.

18:4
The mouth is like the source of a great river;
its words can irrigate or flood.

18:5
Returning kindness for evil is not good,
for how then will you honor kindness?[87]

18:6
Foolish words attract contention;
foolish acts invite violence.

88 Too many of us imagine spirituality to be a feeling or a quality when in fact it is a practice and a discipline. Spiritual people are not limited in their feelings and feel the full range of what we humans can feel. Their discipline isn't in controlling what they feel, but controlling how they act in response to what they feel.

89 Surrendering to God, or better yet, being surrendered to God by God, you no longer imagine you are separate from God or alienated from anyone or anything else. Rather, you draw your strength and endurance from the Whole of which you are a part, and move on.

90 Do not respond to people from the scripts dictated by your philosophy or religion. Rather, listen without a filter to whatever is said, and respond without a prepackaged worldview. In this way you can hear the truth in what is said, and respond honestly as well.

18:7
Foolish words bring disaster
and cause your soul to falter.

18:8
Whining is like a hammer;
its pounding shatters the heart.

18:9
If you are lax in your discipline,
you contribute to your own destruction.[88]

18:10
Surrendering to God is the key to endurance;
this way you will finish the course.[89]

18:11
Do not belittle wealth;
it can be a source of strength in time of trouble.

18:12
The arrogant teeter on the brink of destruction;
the humble stand at the threshold of honor.

18:13
Offering advice before listening carefully
is both stupid and useless.[90]

18:14
A joyous heart strengthens the body;
despair worsens every disease.

91 Carry a coin in your pocket. Whenever you imagine you are undecided upon a course of action, take out the coin and flip it. Heads you will do *x*; tails you will do *y*. When the coin is tossed and the decision is made, what is your gut reaction? If you are troubled by the result, do the opposite. If you are calm in response, follow the coin's advice.

92 This and the previous proverb (along with many others) focus on the power of speech. While actions may speak louder than words, words are often the catalyst for action. Speak cautiously, seeing that your words are true and compassionate even if they must be forceful and critical.

18:15

Intuition is a source of knowledge,
but do not forsake reason in your quest for truth.

18:16

Generosity opens many doors;
even the famous welcome the open-hearted.

18:17

Do not be the first person to complain;
wait until you have heard what others have to say.

18:18

The toss of a coin can sometimes end quarrels
and send the contentious on their way.[91]

18:19

Even quarreling brothers and sisters
will often come to each other's defense.

18:20

The satisfaction of your soul
depends upon the quality of your words.

18:21

Death and life lie in the power of words;
rush to use words and you may be forced to eat them.[92]

18:22

A loving partner is a source of happiness;
God smiles on the union of such souls.

93 Several other proverbs such as "A friend's love is always available, but siblings are there in times of trouble" (17:17) seem to elevate family over friends. This proverb does the opposite. The message overall isn't to value one over the other, but to celebrate those bonds that can weather the storms of hurt. Trust, compassion, respect, and love are the keys to lasting relationships, whether rooted in family or friendship.

94 We often lie to avoid the consequences of telling the truth. But whatever they may be, chances are the consequences of lying are greater still. As is said in recovery programs, "You are only as sick as your secrets." The liar is trapped in a world of fictions that are increasingly difficult to remember. Fear of being caught in a lie is ever present, perverting even those moments when truth is spoken.

18:23
When you ask for a favor, speak gently;
keep your words soft no matter how harsh the response.

18:24
Friends may be closer than siblings,
for friendship rests on a foundation of trust, not blood.[93]

19:1
Better a pauper on the path of innocence
than the rich on the road to corruption.

19:2
Hearts empty of understanding have nothing to offer;
feet that run before the eyes have seen carry you toward evil.

19:3
Ignorance is corrupting;
embrace it and your heart will rage against justice.

19:4
Wealth attracts many followers;
poverty can separate you even from your friends.

19:5
Bearing false witness cannot be excused;
lying invites its own dire consequences.[94]

19:6
The poor are drawn to the generous;
even the wealthy honor one who gives freely.

95   True understanding is knowing that you are part of the greater oneness that is God. Knowing you are divine, and being able to draw from
that infinite source of compassion and justice, raises the self beyond
selfishness and the fear in which selfishness is rooted. Being raised
beyond fear and rooted in love is the ultimate self-esteem.

96   We take offense when we imagine the people offending us could
have done otherwise. But is this so? At the moment of their offense,
were they really free to do other than they did, to say something other
than they said? Do you stand apart from your words and deeds at each
moment and evaluate the consequences before acting or speaking, or
do you just act and speak and then find yourself shocked by the unan-
ticipated and unexpected result? Few of us act and speak with restraint.
Don't expect of others what you cannot do yourself.

19:7
A despairing heart drives away friends;
when it cries out, there is no one to hear.

19:8
True understanding brings self-esteem;
happiness arises in a heart fulfilled.[95]

19:9
A false witness stands self-condemned;
liars are trapped by their own lies.

19:10
Wealth is wasted on the ignorant,
for their desires are insatiable.

19:11
Patience is a sign of intelligence;
honor comes to those who do not take offense.[96]

19:12
The ignorant rampage like young lions;
their attention lasts no longer than dew on grass.

19:13
An unruly child causes heartache;
a nagging spouse is like a dripping tap.

19:14
Property and wealth can be inherited,
but a wise spouse is a gift from God.

97 We have heard something like this before: "Always speak as if talking to God" (16:1). God is all there is. So the wealthy and the poor, the evil and the just, are all God. When you come upon the poor and homeless, do not turn away your gaze, but engage with them as if you were meeting God, for indeed you are. Giving to God in the guise of the poor reminds you that God wears infinite masks. God's Face is every face, even your own. And realizing that is the reward for giving to the poor.

98 We become angry when we don't get our way. But for this to happen we must also hold the belief that we could have gotten our way if someone or something had not intervened. Anger needs the illusion of control, and because control is an illusion, the illusion of control needs the fiction of an enemy seeking to take that control away. It is the enemy that explains the loss of control and allows the illusion to be maintained. If you seek to soothe another's anger, you are only volunteering to hold the place of the enemy. Let the anger burn itself out, and then offer a hand.

99 Reality is reality, and there is nothing you can do about it. Dream all you want, and work hard to achieve whatever it is you dream of achieving, but just do not imagine this will guarantee you success. Variables are innumerable; you cannot account for them all. Thus, make sure the dream is just, the path to it brings you joy, and leave the rest to God.

19:15
Laziness leads to neglect;
idle minds receive no nourishment.

19:16
Doing what needs to be done is a boon to the soul;
ignoring responsibility is the way of death.

19:17
When you give to the poor, imagine you are giving to God;
your reward will be instantaneous.[97]

19:18
Hope requires curbing desire;
Self-indulgence is the path to destruction.

19:19
Angry people cause their own problems;
trying to intervene only fuels their anger.[98]

19:20
Welcome advice and discipline when you are young;
they will bring wisdom when you are older.

19:21
Your mind is filled with many dreams,
yet life unfolds despite them.[99]

19:22
Better to befriend an honest pauper
than kneel before a treacherous king.

100 Everyone makes mistakes, but if your life is marked by goodness, mistakes will be forgiven while you live and forgotten after you die.

101 The wicked may thrive outwardly, but their spirit is constantly vexed with fear. Those who live in a world of distrust can trust no one, and though many may seek their company in order to siphon their wealth, none seek their friendship or offer it to them.

19:23
The key to life is attention to the truth;
the godly die in peace and their mistakes are forgotten.[100]

19:24
You may be holding food in your hand,
but you will starve unless you put it in your mouth.

19:25
Discipline the cynical and they grow clever;
discipline the wise and they grow wiser.

19:26
Security and independence mean nothing
to parents whose children are delinquent.

19:27
Attending to reality returns your feet to the path
and your mind to the present moment.

19:28
A lying witness makes a mockery of justice,
and the mouth of the wicked gorge on crime.

19:29
There is retribution for the wicked,
and every fool will suffer the marks of foolishness.[101]

20:1
Wine loosens the tongue and causes trouble;
this is not the path of discrimination.

[102] Speaking of the Hebrew Bible, the wisdom of living a godly life, Moses says, "Surely, this Instruction which I enjoin upon you this day is not too baffling for you, nor is it beyond reach. It is not in the heavens, that you should say, 'Who among us can go up to the heavens and get it for us and impart it to us, that we may observe it?' Neither is it beyond the sea, that you should say, 'Who among us can cross to the other side of the sea and get it for us and impart it to us, that we may observe it?' No, the thing is very close to you, in your mouth and in your heart, to observe it" (Deuteronomy 30:11–14, JPS). The key is not to seek the truth outside yourself, but to open to the truth implanted within yourself.

[103] Even the wise can make mistakes and cause others harm. Thus, they are always on guard to act wisely. Only the foolish imagine there is a steady state where vigilance is abandoned and goodness happens of its own accord. No matter how wise you are, you never outgrow the need for caution.

20:2
Do not provoke the king's anger;
treat him as you would a raging lion.

20:3
Avoiding an argument is a wise choice;
a hasty retort is a sign of stupidity.

20:4
The lazy shirk their responsibilities when times are hard
and then expect to harvest what they did not sow.

20:5
Understanding is a deep river running through the heart;
learn to draw from it and you will grow wise.[102]

20:6
Most people claim to be kind,
but the truth is known through their deeds.

20:7
Good citizens are full of integrity;
those who follow their leadership are fortunate.

20:8
A discerning mind recognizes what is false
by simply observing the situation.

20:9
There is no permanent state of purity;
do not imagine your heart is pure and your errors erased.[103]

104 There are degrees of hearing and seeing. The fool takes in only what is on the surface; the wise make time to delve deeper.

20:10
Cheating customers and stealing from owners
cheapen the honor of honest labor.

20:11
Youth is no excuse;
goodness and justice are for everyone.

20:12
The ear is for listening, not just hearing;
the eye for seeing, not just looking.[104]

20:13
Those who prefer illusion impoverish their souls;
the awakened eye sees riches wherever it rests.

20:14
Do not complain about how others do business
and then boast to your friends of your own cleverness.

20:15
Gold and pearls are worth nothing
when compared to right speech.

20:16
Obtain collateral from anyone cosigning for a stranger
or vouching for someone you do not know.

20:17
The bread of falsehood tastes sweet at first,
but once chewed it turns to gravel in your mouth.

105 Do not imagine you can withstand the pressure of the crowd. In time, your norms will reflect those of your community. If they value falsehood, you too will come to lie and call it truth. Befriend those who can lift you to higher levels of justice and compassion, not those who seek to bring you to lower ones.

106 It is common to assign all our troubles to our parents, but this is only an excuse for not living rightly. Parents may set the stage of our lives, but they do not determine our actions upon it.

107 Why are you here? What is the purpose of life in general and your life in particular? The purpose of life is to know life itself, and in so doing to know God. When you make your life a journey to God, you will discover that it is in fact a journey with God. Life is God's way of discovering God's own Self. You are the way God does this as you.

20:18
Make sure to seek objective counsel
when planning strategies for success.

20:19
Beware of mingling among the indiscreet
or with those who gossip and tell lies.[105]

20:20
Blaming your parents keeps you from tending your own
    flame;
when night falls, you will be lost in darkness.[106]

20:21
Do not rush to enjoy what comes easily;
make sure the blessing does not disguise a curse.

20:22
Do not dedicate your life to revenge;
surrender your revenge to God.

20:23
Do not deceive those who trust you;
anything less than an honest measure is wrong.

20:24
Each step is taken in the company of God,
if you understand the nature of the journey.[107]

20:25
Injustice and lies lead you from the path;
honesty and generosity return you to it.

108 But to illuminate the darkest recesses of heart and mind, you must be willing to enter into them. If you live life afraid of the shadows, you will live life surrounded by them.

109 We live in a culture that values youth and finds aging an embarrassment. This is the way of the foolish. The wise know that wisdom, like fine wine, needs time to ripen. As we age, the distractions and folly of youth fall away and we are free to live life wisely, with humor, grace, humility, and a joy far richer than the silliness of youth.

110 A farmer waters the crops and wastes no water on that which is not meant to grow. The same with the wise: they water only justice and compassion and let evil shrivel for lack of attention.

20:26
A wise leader knows how to quell troublemakers
and turn their mischief against them.

20:27
The soul is a lamp that illuminates
the darkest corners of mind and heart.[108]

20:28
Kindness and truth sustain you on the path;
through these you will be strengthened.

20:29
The young take pride in their youth,
but the old find value in aging.[109]

20:30
Punishment may reform the criminal,
but the wise are guided by the gnawing of conscience.

21:1
Like a farmer irrigating his fields,
let truth direct the desires of your heart.[110]

21:2
It is easy to rationalize your actions;
look for the truth buried beneath your excuses.

21:3
Doing what is right and just
is true service to God.

111 Perfection is not ours to achieve. We will make mistakes, but if they are honest ones, we can recover quickly and move on.

21:4
A disdainful attitude and a proud heart
sow the seeds of discord.

21:5
Although at the beginning your thoughts are pure and good,
hasty action may result in loss.

21:6
Ill-gotten gains are like poisoned perfume;
attraction to either leads to death.

21:7
Those who are not honest with themselves are like thieves
whose lives are blighted by fear.

21:8
Your actions are sometimes inconsistent and odd;
just be sure they are always straightforward.[111]

21:9
Living alone in the corner of an attic
is better than sharing a large space with a difficult spouse.

21:10
A warped mind looks for trouble;
even friends are sacrificed to achieve its aims.

21:11
Punishment may teach some people,
but the wise gain knowledge through instruction.

112 The wealth of the wicked is ill-gotten, and because it is so, the wicked assume there is an advantage to acting wickedly. One can expect nothing less. The danger is when we begin to think this way as well. There may be short-term benefits to evil, but in the end evil consumes its own.

113 We become angry when we do not get what we desire. Giving to those who have even less than us humbles us and frees us from the conceit of control and the anger that such conceit engenders.

114 Who sets the traps for the righteous? Do not imagine they are set by the wicked. Reality itself sets traps, for rising and falling are part of life and there is no life without both. Yet even these are not set consciously, or deliberately, or with you in mind. Traps are set; people fall into them. But the wise are on the lookout for such traps and avoid most, while the foolish are blind to reality and trip into many.

21:12
Even the wicked prosper;
they credit their good fortune to evil.[112]

21:13
Ignore the cry of the needy
and your own cries will be ignored.

21:14
Giving anonymously to the poor frees you from anger;
generosity is an antidote to wrath.[113]

21:15
Just deeds bring joy
and destroy the workings of iniquity.

21:16
Wander off the path of wisdom
and you will find yourself among dead souls.

21:17
Devoting yourself to pleasure will leave you penniless;
indulge in wine and perfume, and poverty awaits you.

21:18
Traps are set for the righteous,
but it is the wicked who fall into them.[114]

21:19
Better to pitch your tent in a wasteland
than live with a violent and angry spouse.

115 Notice that "strength and honor will follow you." What stays with you is what you do: goodness and kindness; what you leave behind is strength and honor. When you do good and practice kindness you strengthen others and honor them. It is not your strength and honor the sage is talking about, but the strength and honor you instill in others through your acts of goodness and kindness.

116 Strength here is different than in the previous teaching. There, strength is linked to honor, suggesting a sense of self-worth. Here, strength is pitted against wisdom, suggesting two ways of engaging the world. In this proverb, "strength" refers to your efforts to bend reality to your will, while wisdom refers to your capacity to bend in sync with reality. The former always exhausts you; the latter always empowers you.

117 This is why they are called "ignorant": they ignore the fact that we are all part of a singular system. By focusing on self alone, the ignorant create a world of alienation and fear that sacrifices cooperation to competition, and makes true community impossible.

21:20
The wise conserve what they have;
the ignorant squander their inheritance and become poor.

21:21
Do good and be kind,
and strength and honor will follow you.[115]

21:22
The mind controls the body;
place your trust in wisdom, not strength.[116]

21:23
Guard your tongue
and you protect your soul.

21:24
Those who impose their will on others
fall prey to arrogance and evil.

21:25
Laziness will overcome you
if you resist every impulse to work.

21:26
The ignorant dream and accomplish nothing;
The wise act to the benefit of both self and other.

21:27
Whatever the ignorant have to offer
they will use to their own advantage.[117]

118 Lies and gossip have a life of their own. There is a story of a repentant gossip who seeks the advice of his rabbi. "How can I make up for all the hurt I have caused?" he asks. "Go to the market and buy four of the finest feather pillows you can afford. Then take them to the hilltop overlooking our village, slice them open, and scatter the feathers to the wind."

Upon completing the task, the man returns to the rabbi expecting forgiveness.

"Not just yet," the rabbi says. "Now take the empty pillow cases and retrieve all the feathers you have scattered."

"But that is impossible!" the man cries. "They have been carried far beyond my reach!" "The same is true of your lies and gossip. There is no way to make amends for such behavior."

119 The sign of the wise is humility: their wisdom consists in knowing what they don't know and cannot know, and not simply in what they do know. Those who are foolish know very little and imagine that what they do not know is even less.

120 How can you know if your thoughts are wise? Measure the quality of the deeds they propose. If your thoughts promote acts of justice and your feelings promote acts of kindness, your wisdom is secure. If they promote selfish acts and hurtful deeds, you can be certain you are a fool. But only the wise will ever admit it.

121 Wealth or the lack of it isn't a sign of wisdom or godliness. What matters is what the wealthy do with their wealth, and how the poor survive their poverty. God manifests as all reality, so do not imagine the wealthy are rewarded and the poor are punished. God is simply God in every instance. Seeing that in others is a mark of understanding; seeing that in yourself is a mark of wisdom.

21:28
False testimony may be refuted,
but once it is voiced, everyone repeats it.[118]

21:29
Know-it-alls display their ignorance;
the wise trust in not knowing.[119]

21:30
Wisdom and understanding
never recommend ungodly action.[120]

21:31
Saddle your horse for battle,
but never take victory for granted.

22:1
Your good name is your greatest treasure;
your reputation more precious than silver or gold.

22:2
Don't praise the rich nor condemn the poor;
they are both equal in God's eyes.[121]

22:3
The wise recognize trouble and avoid it;
the thoughtless do not notice and pay dearly.

122 Humility must be genuine, that is to say, self-emptying. A false humility, one that bloats the self even as it pretends to deflate it, is a tactic for self-indulgence rather than self-surrender. When you know the truth that all is God, the self-emptying happens of its own accord. You are humbled before all, and open to all, and thus ready to know that God is all.

22:4
Humility brings you into God's presence,
and with this comes wealth, honor, and vitality.[122]

22:5
The path of the ignorant is strewn with thorns and snares;
the wise choose not to walk this way.

22:6
Teach people the truth when they are young,
and they will not abandon it even in old age.

22:7
The rich dominate the poor,
and the debtor is bound to the creditor.

22:8
Sow injustice and reap disaster;
anger will burn up your inheritance.

22:9
Blessed are those who give bread to the poor,
seeing past their poverty to their divinity.

22:10
Put an end to sarcasm and ridicule,
and judgment and shame will also cease.

22:11
One who has a pure heart and kind speech
dwells in the company of God.

123 Laziness is often excused by inflated notions of how difficult a task must be. Imagining something is too difficult for you to accomplish frees you from trying to accomplish it. The wise neither minimize nor inflate the difficulties of life; they simply engage them as best they can.

124 The ultimate truth is ineffable. This doesn't demean speech, but it should humble the speaker. Use words wisely, but never mistake them for the reality toward which they point. You may become stuffed from eating the menu, but nutrition still lies with the meal. Practicing silence allows you to taste the truth, just as eating chocolate reveals far more than chewing on the letters c-h-o-c-o-l-a-t-e.

22:12
God protects knowledge;
honesty reveals the words of the liar.

22:13
The lazy imagine stalking lions
and then cower from their own fantasies.[123]

22:14
The mouth that utters falsehood
will swallow the one who speaks it.

22:15
If you are tied to the illusion of words,
only silence can separate you from it.[124]

22:16
Whatever you think to gain from exploitation
will ultimately be counted as a loss.

1   This is the opening of a new section of teachings, and is made up of two parts: 22:22–23:11 and 23:12–24:22. The first part parallels, and most likely adapts, an older collection of Egyptian wisdom material called the *Instruction of Amen-em-opet*, which was translated into Aramaic in the seventh century BCE. At that time Aramaic was the common language of the Near East, and the Hebrew sages would have been familiar with the book. Admiring its wisdom, they made their own Hebrew translation and included fifteen of its twenty-four teachings in this section of the Book of Proverbs.

2   Repeating proverbs was and is a practical and contemplative practice: practical in the sense that you plant their words in your mind so that they might flower in your actions; contemplative in that they can be used as mantra. As you read through the Thirty Precepts of Wisdom, note those that speak to you most powerfully. Taking up each precept at a time, commit it to memory and repeat it throughout the day, allowing yourself to derive new meaning from it with each repetition. For example, "Do not exploit the defenseless" (22:22): As you examine this teaching throughout the day, continually ask yourself, "Who are the defenseless, and how might I be exploiting them?" As your list of "the defenseless" grows and your understanding of exploitation becomes more nuanced, you will work at deeper and deeper levels of your life to root out this negative trait.

3   The Book of Proverbs seems to align itself with the notion of karma. Actions have consequences: do good, get good; do bad, get bad. Later Hebrew wisdom books such as the Book of Job and Ecclesiastes refute this notion, saying that reality does not conform to our will or deeds.

☐ The Thirty Precepts of Wisdom

Prologue[1]

22:17–21
Concentrate on the words of the wise,
and establish your heart in truth.
Repeating the words of the wise
will protect you from wrong.[2]
Trust in God, even if you feel unworthy.
I will now tell you the path you should follow.
Here I will give you in writing
the thirty principles of knowledge that you need.
I have written down the elements of truth
so that you will be able to teach other seekers.

–1–

22:22–23
Do not exploit the defenseless,
nor take advantage of the poor.
For God will come to their rescue,
stripping from you what you planned to steal from them.[3]

4 | So many of us imagine that the sages of the past lived in an age so different from ours that they have nothing of value to say to us. While it is true that we have progressed in ways they could not imagine—technology—and would not accept—women's suffrage, abolition of slavery, to name but two—it is also true that as a species we are still plagued by the same emotions such as arrogance, hatred, fear, and jealousy. While we need not imitate their Bronze Age biases, we can benefit from their attempts to tame the demons that haunt us to this day.

–2–

22:24–25
Do not entertain anger
or be tempted by rage.
The more you lose your temper,
the more you become its slave.

–3–

22:26
Do not rush to make a deal
or guarantee a loan.
If you cannot afford to lose money,
do not risk the very bed you sleep on.

–4–

22:27–28
Do not discount the wisdom of the past;
it may save you from traps in the present.[4]

–5–

22:29
A hard worker can stand tall before kings;
there is no greater honor than honest labor.

5 There are people who, masquerading as do-gooders, seek only to control you. Be careful when accepting the largesse of others, and make sure that their gifts are free and not laden with strings thick enough to bind you.

–6–

23:1–3
Be wary when dining with the powerful;
think carefully before opening your mouth.
If it helps, imagine a knife at your throat
and keep your appetite under your control.
Don't envy their rich food,
for their cake may be laced with deceit.

–7–

23:4–5
Do not berate yourself for having less;
take comfort in your own understanding.
Money comes when it comes and then disappears,
like an eagle soaring high in the heavens.

–8–

23:6–8
Do not break bread with the mean-spirited,
nor envy their possessions.
They will tally up each mouthful of food.
Eat! Drink! they insist, but they don't really mean it.
Their bread will turn in your stomach,
and they will use your expressions of thanks to strangle you.[5]

6 Wisdom is to be shared, but if the person with whom you wish to share isn't listening, you are wasting your breath. Only offer what you know when the time is right and the person to whom you offer it is ready to receive. Forcing your wisdom on another only shows that you are not all that wise.

7 Compare this proverb to Genesis 8:21, "For the inclination of the human heart is evil from youth." What is meant by "youth"? Youth in both of these texts refers to that period when the ego is coming into its own, and with it sexual desire. The temptations of youth are driven by hormones flooding the brain. Learning to discipline these desires from the beginning allows you to mature in a more sane manner, freeing you from youthful mistakes that can mar a lifetime of good deeds.

8 How do you know if you are wise? People find joy and comfort in your company. If you are alone and lonely, do not assume others are not ready for your wisdom. Think instead that you may not be all that wise.

–9–

23:9
Don't waste your words on those who plug their ears;
they will not value what you have to say.[6]

–10–

23:10–12
Do not steal from the defenseless;
they are protected by God.
Open your heart to correction
and your ears to knowledge.

–11–

23:13–14
Do not give in to the temptations of your youth;
discipline will not kill you.
Make every effort to resist
and keep your soul from lasting guilt.[7]

–12–

23:15–16
A wise heart brings joy to others;
they will yearn for your good counsel.[8]

9 Being mindful of God translates into godliness: acts of justice and compassion. Faith here does not mean belief. Having faith in godliness isn't believing in justice and compassion but acting justly and compassionately.

10 This teaching originally appears in the middle of the following one, breaking up the parallel verses referring to father and mother. I have moved it to allow the intended parallel to present itself more clearly.

11 The wisdom of the sages is not for sale. Those who market wisdom as one might sell fruits and vegetables are making a mockery of learning. The wisdom of the sages is given freely to all who wish to receive it. While it may be that the wealthy can support the wise and free them for learning, one who makes a living from wisdom is exploiting the ignorance of others rather than ending it.

–13–

23:17–18
Do not envy those who worship pleasure;
try to be mindful of God all day.
Godliness is all that lasts;
faith in it is never misplaced.[9]

–14–

23:19–21
Listen to me and grow wise;
follow what you know in your heart.
Do not go out drinking every night,
nor keep company with the greedy.
Wine and meat will drain your reserves,
and drowsiness will overcome you.

–15–

23:23[10]
By all means get truth,
but do not reduce wisdom, discipline, and understanding to
    commodities.[11]

12 The parallel "listen to your father" and "honor your mother" suggests that listening and honoring are, in this proverb, one and the same. When you listen to your father, you honor him; you honor your mother by listening to her. Listening is not the same as abiding, however, and it may be that what you hear from your mother and father is not wisdom. This is why what makes father happy and mother rejoice (again happiness and rejoicing are considered synonymous here) isn't that you do what they say, but that you become wise. While the advice and admonitions of parents may be intended for wisdom, you will have to determine their level of wisdom for yourself.

13 Both lust and evil passion entrap you, but each does so its own way. Lust limits your capacity to think. Evil passion narrows your choice of action. When you lust for something, nothing else matters but that thing—you fall into a deep and deepening pit of obsession. When you give in to evil passion (passion for self at the expense of others), your behavioral choices are narrowed by greater and greater degrees of selfishness. The wise are free to think broadly and do creatively, the wicked can do neither.

–16–

23:22, 23:24–25
Always listen to your father,
and honor your mother no matter how old she grows.[12]
The father of the wise is happy;
the mother of the wise rejoices.
Become wise and those who raised you will celebrate.

–17–

23:26–28
Turn your heart to wisdom
and your eyes will be drawn to the good.
Lust is a deep pit, and evil passion a narrow well—
fall into either one and you are trapped.[13]

14 The wise engage reality; the foolish deny it. This is why the foolish are always arguing, babbling, and battling—not to improve reality, but to maintain their alternatives to it. They turn to drink not to excuse their behavior, but to prevent themselves from having to admit the madness of their fantasies. This is true of all distractive behaviors. We watch "reality TV," for example, not to see what is real, but to avoid what is real.

15 The "mischief makers" are the arguers, babblers, and combatants of the previous proverb. What they are disconnected from is reality. The mischief they stir up is to confuse those who admire them regarding what is true, factual, and real. The mischief makers mistake facts for what they believe, truth for what they believe most passionately, and reality for what they believe most loudly.

–18–

23:29–35

Observe those who are devoted
to quarreling, idle talk, and fighting.
They linger over wine
and indulge themselves with strong liquor.
You will not discover truth at the bottom of a wineglass.
An alcoholic loses his grasp on reality
as surely as death comes from a sudden snakebite.
If you drink like this, you will hallucinate and the world will
     appear distorted.
Everything will lurch up and down like a raft on the high
     seas.
You claim that wine is medicine,
that it will be your salvation,
but when you are sober, you will long for more wine
and the madness you now call sanity.[14]

–19–

24:1–2

Do not admire mischief makers, nor seek out their
     company.[15]
They are up to no good and are always discontented.

16 Tranquility, the capacity to accept what is without the suffering that arises when you insist it be other than it is, is the gift of wisdom. A person who claims to be wise and yet is continually anxious is not wise. Look to the quality of a teacher's life, and not solely to the beauty of her words.

17 Your mind is seduced by selfish desires that isolate you from others as they compel you to pursue private gain at others' expense. Any goal that is achieved only at the expense of the innocent is a goal driven by folly, not wisdom.

–20–

24:3–4

A true home is built on wisdom, with a firm foundation of
understanding.
Knowledge gives each room a deep tranquility.[16]

–21–

24:5–6

The wise are steadfast and fortified by knowledge.
Their plans come to fruition, and their counsel is useful.

–22–

24:7

To the ignorant, wisdom makes no sense;
they do not know enough to ask for help.

–23–

24:8–9

Allow your mind to be seduced, and you will make mistakes.
Distraction leads away from truth; cynicism will cripple
you.[17]

–24–

24:10

Do not plead weakness when someone needs you;
eventually your own strength will fail you.

18 This and the preceding proverb speak to the interdependence of life. Self-reliance is not the same as self-sufficiency. We need to do what we can for ourselves, but there are things that require the help of others. Help when asked and you will be helped when in need. And advocate for justice even when not asked, for when injustice rules, you will not be spared through quiescence.

19 The wise know that the wicked act from ignorance. Had the wicked known the interconnectedness of all life, they would have seen the harm they were about to do and refrained from doing it. Ignorant of this, they know neither God—the source and substance of this interconnected reality—nor godliness, the way to live in it justly and kindly. Thus the wise find no joy in the imprisonment of the wicked, though they understand its necessity.

–25–

24:11–12
If innocent people are murdered and you do nothing,
it is no good pleading ignorance.
God sees the situation clearly.
The moment will come when you are in danger,
and your inaction will be repaid by the inaction of others.[18]

–26–

24:13–14
You eat honey for its simple goodness
and its sweet taste on your tongue.
So let it be with wisdom,
for it, too, is good and offers you the sweetness of hope.

–27–

24:15–16
Wickedness disturbs tranquility.
Goodness may fall seven times, but recovers eight;
evil stumbles once and is destroyed.

–28–

24:17–18
Do not gloat when criminals are caught and punished.
Their punishment is not for your pleasure,
and your enjoyment may change the course of events.[19]

20 Unable to choose piety over power, the foolish follow the mighty rather than the wise. Following the way of power leads to acts of exploitation, and acts of exploitation will eventually bring the foolish to ruin—whether at the hands of God or kings, one cannot always tell. Ruin that comes from God can be likened to a person who drills a hole in the bottom of his boat hoping to drown his fellow passengers. As they drown, so does he. Ruin that comes from kings is like a person who assists the king in plundering another kingdom and whom the king then murders rather than pay him his share. In the former, reality itself leads to his end. In the latter, the wickedness of the king simply overwhelms his own.

–29–

24:19–20
Do not rail against the wicked,
nor envy what they do.
They leave nothing behind,
and their lamp is extinguished forever.

–30–

24:21–22
Respect both God and king,
but choose the former over the latter.
Do not trust those who cannot decide between piety and
     power;
calamity fells them suddenly,
and who knows whether this comes from God or king?[20]

1 This line introduces yet another, albeit very short, collection of proverbs. They are not attributed to Solomon per se, but were thought to have been collected by him.

2 Justice in the courts is essential to a just society. If the judges are corrupt, excusing evil rather than punishing it, the nation cannot stand long.

3 A judge should take no delight in sentencing the guilty. While society must be protected from the wicked, the fact that such people exist should lead us to sadness, not joy.

☐ Sayings of Solomon's Contemporaries

24:23
These, too, are the sayings of the wise:[1]
If you have to make a judgment, show no favoritism.

24:24
Those who judge the guilty as innocent will be shunned,
and everyone will avoid their company.[2]

24:25
If you have to sentence someone, do it firmly but kindly,
and you will be respected.[3]

24:26
Always speak honestly and directly,
and people will receive what you say as though it were a kiss.

24:27
Before embarking on family life,
make sure that you can afford to support those you will
    come to love.

4 | Nothing comes to those who wait, or at least not to those who wait too long. It isn't that the idle do not have fields but that they do not tend to them, imagining that they will somehow take care of themselves. But entropy is the law, and all things give way to chaos unless continually refreshed. Do not imagine the wise avoid work or that labor is beneath them. On the contrary, the wise know when to work, while the foolish know nothing of it.

24:28
Do not let your feelings for one friend
persuade you to betray another.

24:29
Do not feel indebted
to one who cheats on your behalf.

24:30–31
What does laziness accomplish?
Look at the fields and vineyards of the idle.
They are overgrown with thistles,
the ground is covered with nettles, stone walls no longer
     stand.

24:32–34
Observe this and see what it teaches you.
The lazy curl up in bed: a little more sleep, another short nap;
poverty sneaks up on them, and robs them of all they have.[4]

1 Hezekiah was king of Judah during the last thirty years of the eighth century BCE. His scribes would have collected the wisdom of the past and, as per tradition, ascribed the sayings to Solomon. Whether or not Solomon is the author of them is undeterminable.

2 Myth, metaphor, and parable are the way spiritual truths are communicated. They point to truths beyond themselves, and the wise are careful not to mistake the words for the thing to which they point. In matters of law and governance, metaphor and myth are a needless abstraction, and the wise seek to articulate laws unambiguously.

☐ The Second Collection of Shorter Sayings

25:1
Here are further sayings of Solomon
collected by the scribes of Hezekiah, king of Judah.[1]

25:2
In matters of the spirit, metaphor is used;
in matters of state, it is better to speak plainly.[2]

25:3
As unfathomable as heaven's height and earth's depth
is the heart of a wise leader.

25:4–5
Just as dross must be removed from silver
before it can be refined into a cup,
so wickedness must be driven from a nation
if its leaders are to govern with integrity.

25:6–7
Do not boast to curry favor with the powerful.
Let them invite you to join them of their own accord.
If you overstate your case, you may be demoted later.

3 While the powerful may not be wise, their power alone is to be respected, for it can cause you great harm. Be careful when dealing with people more powerful than you; do not provoke them, but understand that power in the hands of fools only makes them more foolish. Keep your distance if you can; hold your tongue if you cannot.

25:8
Do not get involved in an argument
unless the whole matter is clear.

25:9–10
Do not betray a confidence in the heat of the moment;
you may be overheard and lose your reputation forever.

25:11
Like golden apples engraved on silver plates
is a well-timed word of advice.

25:12
Like a nose ring of gold or a precious brooch
is wise counsel in a receptive ear.

25:13
Like cooling snow during winter's harvest,
one who keeps a promise refreshes the spirit.

25:14
Like empty clouds and hot dry winds
is one whose promises are hollow.

25:15
Do not be impatient with the powerful;
respond gently to their anger.[3]

25:16
When you find honey, eat only what you need;
any more will sour your stomach.

4 Vinegar removed the bitterness and acidity of ancient wines. Just so, a song of joy or word of wise comfort can soften the bitterness of heartache.

5 More a matter of "killing with kindness" than "love your enemies" (Matthew 5:44; Luke 6:27 and 6:35), the hope of the sage here is to change another's mind by refusing to treat the other as an enemy.

25:17
Tread softly in a friend's house,
for even friendship has its limits.

25:18
False testimony is as deadly
as any weapon.

25:19
Like a broken tooth or sprained ankle
is trust betrayed in a time of need.

25:20
Like a thin cloak in winter, or wine mixed with vinegar,
is a song of joy to a saddened heart.[4]

25:21–22
If your enemy is hungry—bring food. If thirsty—bring water.
Your actions may shame your adversary into a change of
    heart.[5]

25:23
As sure as the north wind brings rain,
slander calls forth anger.

25:24
Better to live in the corner of the attic
than deal with an angry spouse among friends.

25:25
Like cold water to a thirsty traveler
is good news from a distant land.

6 Similar to Proverb 25:16, we are reminded that the way of the sage is the way of moderation. It is easy to see how too much honey can make you ill, but too much honor? The problem here is that you may inadvertently trigger the jealousy of others who will do whatever they can to lessen your status and cloak you in dishonor. Thus it is better to practice humility than bask in notoriety no matter how well deserved.

7 While being polite is not the same as humoring someone, be careful that your desire not to shame others isn't mistaken for agreeing with them. State your positions clearly and kindly, and free yourself from the foolish as quickly as you can.

8 While it is useless to insist that the foolish see things as you do, it is also unwise to appear to see things as they do. If there is common ground between you, stand on it, but make sure it isn't ignorance that you share.

25:26
Like a muddied spring or poisoned well
is one who fails to withstand corruption.

25:27
Honey and honor are both sweet,
but too much of either will make you sick.[6]

25:28
Like a city whose walls lie in ruin
is one whose desires are not curbed.

26:1
Like summer snow and winter rain,
honors showered on the ignorant wreak havoc.

26:2
Like a swallow flying back to its nest,
harsh words will haunt their author.

26:3
A whip for the horse, a bridle for the donkey,
and a sharp reproof for the fool.

26:4
Do not humor the ignorant,
or you will appear as witless as they do.[7]

26:5
Answer a fool according to his foolishness,
and he may mistake his ignorance for wisdom.[8]

9 Along with proverbs, parables are a major teaching tool of the wise. But do not imagine that every story contains a wise core. Anyone can tell a parable; only those of the wise lift you to a new way of seeing. The parables of the foolish only excuse more foolishness (see 26:9).

10 This proverb is not meant to endorse dishonoring the ignorant, however. The proper attitude to the ignorant is to offer them the opportunity to become wise. Neither honor nor dishonor should come into play here.

11 Neither God nor the universe revolves around you, and not every event in your life is a "lesson." Spending time trying to fathom why this or that has happened to you robs you of precious moments to respond and move on.

12 So much of what we fear is a product of our own imaginations conjured up to excuse us from doing what needs to be done. Before succumbing to your fears, make sure they are real.

26:6
Sending messages through fools
results in confusion, anger, and misunderstanding.

26:7
A parable from the lips of the ignorant
is as useless as shoes on a man without legs.[9]

26:8
Honoring the ignorant is like loading a stone into a sling:
disaster is bound to follow.[10]

26:9
A thorn in the hand of a drunk causes as much trouble
as a parable told by a fool.

26:10
An undisciplined boss creates confusion
by hiring unqualified and dishonest people.

26:11
Like a dog sniffing its own vomit
is someone who keeps repeating his own mistakes.[11]

26:12
Better to believe you are ignorant
than to convince yourself you are wise.

26:13
The lazy invent excuses to avoid work:
How can I go out? A lion is loose upon the streets.[12]

13 Honoring the lives of others means not meddling in their affairs. If a friend or loved one solicits your advice, listen carefully and respond kindly. But if you are not invited into another's affairs, do not presume you have any reason to intrude.

14 Hiding behind false humor, the wicked seek to find where you are vulnerable. If another hurts you and takes refuge in humor rather than taking responsibility and asking for forgiveness, beware this person and keep your distance.

15 The wicked like it when others are in turmoil, for they see this as an opportunity for advancement at others' expense. When you encounter those who fan the flames of discord, know you are witnessing evil.

26:14
As a door turns on its hinge,
so the lazy turn on their beds.

26:15
The lazy cannot feed themselves
even when the food is placed in their hands.

26:16
The ignorant believe themselves wiser
than seven others with more knowledge than them.

26:17
Like a person pinching the ear of an angry dog
is one who gets embroiled in another's quarrel.[13]

26:18
Like a warrior probing for an army's weakness
is one who lies and says, *I'm only joking*.[14]

26:19
Wood feeds fire,
and sharp words fuel an argument.

26:20
Like a flame to dying embers
is a troublemaker to a cooling temper.[15]

26:21
The words of a complainer
churn the stomachs of those to whom they speak.

16 This and the preceding four proverbs address the capacity of the wicked to deceive people through speech. Do not imagine you can always see through the cunning talk of the wicked. Look instead to their actions and the result of their actions. Words accompanied by good deeds can be trusted; those accompanied by evil deeds are to be dismissed. Actions that appear good and result in goodness are to be trusted. Actions that appear benign but result in hurt are to be condemned.

17 Here again we see the world of the sages: life is so constructed that evil deeds will bring evil to those who do them. This is a comforting notion to many, but for others it appears Pollyannaish at best. The Books of Job and Ecclesiastes, also part of the Hebrew wisdom literature, offer a very different view.

18 Responding to another's hatred or anger with hatred or anger of your own is like throwing gasoline on a fire. Although there is no guarantee that kindness and compassion will douse the flames, they will certainly not feed them.

26:22
Like cheap spoons covered with silver plate
are kind words concealing mean intentions.

26:23
Deceitful words pretend to honesty,
but secretly they harbor fraud.

26:24
The speech of the untrustworthy may be gentle,
but their hearts are hard with malice.

26:25
No matter how pleasant the voice,
look to deeds when deciding whom to trust.[16]

26:26
Though criminals may nurse their grievances in private,
their anger is revealed in public.

26:27
Set a trap and you will be caught in it;
roll a stone to crush another and it will fall on you.[17]

26:28
Hatred feeds upon hatred;
respond gently and hatred may soften.[18]

19 Life is fundamentally uncertain. No matter how good you are, no matter how wise you are, no matter how generous you are—bad things still happen. You cannot earn your way out of the contingencies of life. Doing good, despite those proverbs to the contrary, is no guarantee of getting good. What, then, is the value of goodness? Doing good strengthens the bonds between you and others so that when you are in need they will come to your aid, just as you came to them in their time of trouble.

20 Envy is the most difficult of the negative emotions to uproot because it is rooted in a lack of self-worth. One who is happy with who she is feels no resentment or envy of others. She doesn't compare herself to anyone, but seeks only to be her best. One who is unhappy with who she is, is envious of everyone. This will not change no matter how well she does, for she always belittles herself. If you wish to put an end to envy, seek to discover and cherish your own gifts.

21 The mind has no nest per se, that is, no place in which it can feel safe and find rest. The mind must find safety and rest in itself. A mind at peace with itself is at rest wherever it is, with whatever it observes. Just as the sky is not troubled by the clouds, no matter how dense and dark, so the tranquil mind is untroubled by the most inane thoughts and inappropriate feelings.

27:1
Do not be certain of tomorrow;
no one knows what the future will bring.[19]

27:2
Let your praise come from others, not yourself;
from strangers and not from your own lips.

27:3
A boulder is heavy, and sacks of sand are hard to lift,
but senseless anger weighs more than both.

27:4
Hatred breeds cruelty, and rage smolders,
but envy is the hardest to uproot.[20]

27:5
Even a public rebuke is acceptable
if you know it is coming from love.

27:6
Criticism from a friend is useful,
while support by an enemy is useless.

27:7
A tranquil mind curbs desire;
a disturbed mind mistakes even the bitter for the sweet.

27:8
Like a bird forced from its nest
is a mind unable to be tranquil.[21]

22 While it may seem good to praise others, be careful in whose company you do so. There are those who envy the praise of others and will make it their goal to bring them down rather than legitimately raise themselves up.

27:9
Perfume and incense gladden the heart,
but not as much as the counsel of a good friend.

27:10
Do not forsake your friends,
nor the friends of your parents.
Do not seek help from a sibling far away;
a close neighbor is as good as a distant relative.

27:11
A child's wisdom gladdens a parent's heart
and staves off all humiliation.

27:12
A shrewd person sees trouble coming and avoids it;
the ignorant walk right into it and pay the price.

27:13
Seek collateral from those
who cosign for strangers and foreigners.

27:14
One who talks about others' generosity
invites thieves into his house.[22]

27:15
Living with a crabby spouse is like being locked in a room
with a leaky roof on a rainy day.

23 The role of a friend, partner, or spouse is to be an *ezer k'negdo* (Genesis 2:18). Often translated as "helpmeet" or "fitting helper," the Hebrew original is more provocative. *Ezer* does mean "helper," but *k'negdo* means "over and against." That is, a true friend is one who helps you by pushing you to be better than you currently are. A good friend, spouse, or partner sees the best *you* that you can become and isn't reticent about pointing out when you fail to achieve your own potential. While often painful to hear, their guidance challenges you to greatness and comes only from love.

24 To see your face reflected in water, the water itself must be calm and you must draw close to it. To let your heart mirror the face of a friend, you must be calm and open enough to allow the other to draw near.

25 It is easy for us to say we value what we are taught, but our words often fail to match our actions. If you want to know what you truly value, see what you do and examine what you own. Go through your possessions and consider giving them away, one at a time. Many of the things you own mean nothing to you, and passing them on can be a blessing to you and the one who receives them. But those things from which you cannot part reveal your true values. What are they? What do they say about you?

27:16
Denying your spouse's anger is as impossible
as ignoring the wind or concealing the aroma of a perfumed
hand.

27:17
As iron sharpens iron,
so friends sharpen the minds of friends.[23]

27:18
Whoever cares for a fig tree eats of its fruit,
so one who guards a friend's reputation is also honored.

27:19
As water reflects back your face,
let your heart mirror the face of a friend.[24]

27:20
Like graveyards and hell,
the wandering eye is never satisfied.

27:21
As a refining pot clarifies silver, and a crucible purifies gold,
so what you value reveals your true nature.[25]

27:22
Even if the ignorant were grain,
no mortar and pestle could grind their ignorance out of them.

27:23
Get to know those who work for you,
and delegate responsibility only to those you trust.

26 Again we find a teaching that challenges the "do good, get good" notion of other proverbs in this collection. The wise are not of one mind, only one heart. Where they may differ as to the nature of reward and punishment, they agree as to the value of goodness, compassion, and justice. In this teaching, we are reminded once again that all things come to all people, and that the wise do not bemoan the moments of drought and barrenness, but wait patiently for these to pass, as all moments must.

27 It is important that we distinguish between self-reliance and self-sufficiency. Do what you can for yourself, but know that you cannot survive without the help of others. Allow others to do what they can for themselves, but be ever ready to help when they reach their limits.

28 The ignorant are like people walking through a dark room littered with objects; tripping over the objects is inevitable. The wise walk the same room but carry a lantern that allows them to sidestep the most dangerous threats. The room is the same, but the way each navigates it differs greatly.

27:24
Strength does not last forever,
nor wealth outlive its heirs.

27:25
Know that both profit and loss come to all who labor;
sometimes the mountains bloom, sometimes the hills are
    barren.[26]

27:26
Let your own effort clothe you;
value your labor as you would a prized possession.[27]

27:27
Do not spend more than you can afford,
and do not marry off your children for profit.

28:1
The ignorant run from imagined fears,
while the wise are as confident as strong lions.[28]

28:2
Greedy developers exploit the land;
good citizens preserve it.

28:3
A poor man who robs the destitute
is like a monsoon that destroys the crops.

28:4
Those who forsake wisdom side with the ignorant,
but the wise stand against them.

29 The foolish do not set out to be fools, nor do they necessarily intend to do evil. They simply do what they do without thinking through the consequences. The wise know that even the best intentions can backfire and thus look to potential problems even the kindest act might engender.

30 In accordance with the notion that actions reap their own rewards, the wicked who exploit the poor will find their wealth transferred to the generous who befriend them. How this might happen, the sages don't say. That it must happen is central to their sense of justice.

31 And yet they do succeed! This proverb challenges the notion of "do good, get good; do bad, get bad." Yet there is still a difference between the success of the good and the success of the wicked. The good succeed without exploitation of others, and hence others do not resent their success but applaud it. The wicked succeed only at the expense of others, and only angry silence greets their success.

28:5
Ignorance blinds us to the consequences of our actions;
wisdom opens everything to understanding.[29]

28:6
Better the poor who are innocent
than the rich who twist the ways of justice.

28:7
Those who honor wisdom honor their parents;
those who become drunkards humiliate them.

28:8
The profits of a loan shark
will end up in the pockets of the generous.[30]

28:9
The prayers of those deaf to wisdom
fall on deaf ears.

28:10
Trip up those who are honest, and you yourself will stumble.
The inheritance of innocence is goodness.

28:11
Wealthy people who become self-satisfied
are poorer than those who possess only self-knowledge.

28:12
When the good triumph, there is great rejoicing;
when the wicked succeed, no one applauds.[31]

32 As 12-step recovery people say, "You are only as sick as your secrets." Living without secrets allows you to live without having to cover your tracks and hedge your words. Free from lies, you are free to live more freely.

28:13
Hide your wrongdoing and you will be exposed;
repent your mistakes and you will be forgiven.[32]

28:14
The wise avoid mistakes by taking thought;
the self-important rush toward disaster.

28:15
Like a roaring lion and an angry bear,
the wicked attack the defenseless.

28:16
An ignorant prince invites invasion;
a wise leader governs in peace.

28:17
A murderer will run until exhausted;
no one will offer sanctuary.

28:18
The innocent are saved by their simplicity;
the devious are entrapped by their own cunning.

28:19
Work the land and harvest bread;
pursue vanity and harvest stones.

28:20
A life of integrity is its own blessing;
those impatient for success will end up with nothing.

33 The law alone may not be sufficient to determine guilt and innocence. The wise look beyond the rules to the context in which they are applied.

34 Remember a true friend is an *ezer k'negdo*, one who helps you by challenging you to be the best you can be. A flatterer is satisfied with who you are; a friend seeks to help you become so much more.

35 A child's job is to see to his parents' welfare, not to see how he can use his parents' welfare to see to his own.

36 The abundance spoken of here is not necessarily material abundance, but an abundance of tranquility and peace. The greedy are never satisfied with what they have and are ever troubled by the pursuit of more. The wise are always satisfied with what they have and never seek more at the cost of their own calm.

28:21
Take great care in judging innocence and guilt;
the hungry may steal bread in order to live.[33]

28:22
The eye of the greedy is blind
and cannot discern what is to come.

28:23
The wise know who their friends are:
the counselors, not the flatterers.[34]

28:24
Children who steal from their parents claiming it is their
    inheritance
are no better than criminals.[35]

28:25
The greedy are rewarded with trouble;
those who trust in truth have abundance.[36]

28:26
The ignorant trust their every desire;
the wise escape calamity through discrimination.

28:27
One who gives generously receives generously;
one who ignores the poor courts disaster.

28:28
When the wicked rule, people hide;
when they are overthrown, the righteous inherit.

| 37 | The easiest people to deceive are those whose lives are rooted in deceit. Those who flatter others are prone to flattery themselves. We naturally seek in return that which we give. Be careful that what you give is what you really hope to get.

29:1
The arrogant ignore every warning;
they break their necks because of their rigid position.

29:2
Happiness abounds when the righteous rule,
but misery is audible in the land of the wicked.

29:3
Seekers of wisdom are a blessing to their family;
lovers of sex will squander their inheritance.

29:4
Justice establishes a nation;
graft destroys it.

29:5
Deceive someone by flattery
and you will be deceived in the same manner.[37]

29:6
The wicked are ensnared by their own schemes;
the good sing and are glad.

29:7
The righteous attend to the needs of the poor;
the wicked have no comprehension of justice.

29:8
Mockery can inflame a city,
but the wise know how to cool anger.

38 Heartlessness is the hidden danger in all philosophies that assume one's fate is in one's hands. Those who believe that the quality of our lives depends on the quality of our thoughts—that to think rich is to get rich, and to think poor is to be poor—will come to blame the poor for their poverty, and do nothing to correct an exploitative economic system that makes poverty not only possible but also necessary.

39 Cultivating wisdom is not a matter of memorizing proverbs. Cultivating wisdom requires you to master your impulses and bring your behavior into harmony with justice and compassion. This is hard work, which is why few seek wisdom and content themselves with indulgent fantasies instead.

29:9
The wise who argue with fools
find that neither anger nor humor can resolve the matter.

29:10
The violent despise the innocent;
the wise seek their company.

29:11
The ignorant express their anger;
the wise know how to hold their tongues.

29:12
When an employer is open to gossip,
every employee becomes a tattletale.

29:13
The greedy ignore the poor and the broken,
pretending their fate is the will of God.[38]

29:14
A leader who treats the destitute fairly
will be remembered by posterity.

29:15
Discipline results in wisdom;
self-indulgence is a disgrace to the whole family.[39]

40 While it is true that the wicked prosper for a time, it is also true that over time they fall before the power of truth, righteousness, and wisdom.

41 Knowing you have a harmful habit is the first step in breaking it, but knowledge alone will not change it. Change requires effort: first the effort to resist the impulse, second the effort to replace it with right action. It isn't enough not to do what is evil; you must "turn from evil and do good" (Psalm 34:14).

29:16
Though the wicked may prosper from their wickedness,
the righteous will outlast them.[40]

29:17
Teaching your children self-control
will bring peace and delight to your heart.

29:18
Without vision a nation disintegrates,
but those who adhere to truth are praised.

29:19
Words alone can't bring self-control;
understanding is not enough to break a bad habit.[41]

29:20
There is more hope for a fool
than for those who act without thinking.

29:21
Indulge your desires in your youth
and they will enslave you in old age.

29:22
Anger provokes violence;
uncontrolled rage destroys all hope of reconciliation.

29:23
Pride brings you low;
humility raises you up.

42 The sages are very aware of the influence others can have on you. The norms of your friends become your norms. This is true in all matters of life: If your friends are heavier than you and have no desire to diet, you will have a more difficult time losing weight. If your friends are more well read than you, you will be motivated to read more. Surround yourself with those who are wise, just, and kind and you will find yourself desiring these traits for yourself.

43 The safety spoken of here may not mean that no suffering befalls you. As Job (2:10) and Jesus (Matthew 5:25) tell us, suffering comes to the righteous and the wicked. So what is the safety the wise can expect? The safety of the wise is the surety that suffering will not rob them of tranquility. When challenged by his wife to curse God and die, the beleaguered Job says, "Shall we not accept evil from God as well as good?" God is reality, and reality contains all things and their opposites. Expecting a life free from suffering, the foolish are forever vexed by the suffering they endure, worrying about its cause and seeking to blame others for it. Knowing that suffering as well as joy is part of life, the wise suffer without the added pain of seeking explanations and making excuses. They simply suffer and move on, knowing that this too shall pass.

29:24
Side with thieves and your conscience will be stolen;
even in court you may lie.[42]

29:25
If you fear others, your fear will entrap you;
if you trust in God, you will be safe.[43]

29:26
Many curry favor with the rich,
but true judgment comes from God.

29:27
Criminals are anathema to the law-abiding;
they who are honest are an affront to those who break the law.

1 Most English translations of Proverbs render this verse something like this: "The words of Agur son of Yaqeh; a prophecy to Ithiel, to Ithiel and Ucal." The names Agur, Ithiel, and Ucal appear nowhere else in the Bible. They may not be names at all. *Agur* is the Hebrew word for "collector" and may refer to Solomon, who collected all these proverbs. *Ithiel* may be read as "God is with me," and *Ucal* may mean "I am able." My own sense is that they are indeed titles, but not references to Solomon. Agur the Collector is the collector of doubts who spreads false oracles. The author of this section of Proverbs uses the Doubter to set off the next set of wisdom teachings.

2 The tone here foreshadows that of Ecclesiastes, a far more skeptical book than Proverbs, and attributed to Solomon in his old age. The centuries that separate the writing of the two books makes Solomon's authorship highly unlikely.

□ Warnings and Numerical Proverbs

30:1–4

These are the words of the Doubter to those who are unsure
    of God:[1]

There is no God and we can know nothing of godliness.
We are mere beasts, lacking any understanding.
We have not mastered wisdom nor are we privy to divine revelation.
Who among us can ascend to heaven and return with wisdom?
Who can gather the wind in the palm of a hand?
Who can catch up the waters in a cloak?
Who can set the boundaries of the earth?
What is this person's name?
Does she have children? What are their names?
Tell if you know![2]

(continued on page 221)

3 I have added this line to underline my suggestion that this section is a response to the previous one. The author of this portion of the Book of Proverbs uses the Doubter as a "straw man" against which to promote his wisdom teachings.

4 The references to God are unusual in the Book of Proverbs. The wisdom of the sages is conventional and observable by anyone who takes the time to examine life closely. Wisdom is not a revelation from God, but a result of human investigation. The focus on God suggests that this section is more prophecy than proverb, a spontaneous and ecstatic utterance coming from a sense of closeness to God rather than a careful examination of life.

5 This is a wonderful definition of what it is to be wicked: you mistreat your parents, you are full of yourself, you disdain other people, your speech is devoted to the destruction of other people, and the policies that result from your opinions increase injustice and rob the poor of what little they have.

6 Greed is the surest pathway to dying even while still alive. Driven by insatiable greed, life is never satisfying and lived so poorly that it is a kind of death.

30:5–9

[These are the words of the Knower:][3]
Every word I speak is honed by God.
God is my shield from delusion.
I warn you: do not add to the word of God;
your lies will be tested and exposed.
I ask of God but two things,
may they be granted before I die:
keep me from vanity and falsehood, wealth and poverty;
provide me with a little bread each day,
just enough to sustain me.
Any more and I may imagine it my own doing;
any less and I might turn to theft and lies.[4]

30:10–14

Speak no slander—not even against the wicked
who curse their fathers and neglect their mothers;
who believe themselves to be so pure that they fail to cleanse
   their hearts;
whose eyes blaze with disdain and whose brows arch with
   ridicule;
whose teeth are swords and knives devouring the land of the
   poor
and depriving the destitute of sanctuary.
For so poisonous is slander that in the end it is you that is
   called wicked.[5]

30:15A

Death has two insatiable daughters: Give Me and Give Me.[6]

(continued on page 223)

7 Mirroring Proverb 30:15b–16, this proverb speaks not of those four things that are never satisfied, but of those four things that are beyond comprehension. These four call forth awe in us: the soaring of an eagle, the gliding of a snake, the smooth sailing of a ship, and the wild embrace of lovers. The meaning is this: just as there are passions that cultivate greed and through greed death, there are other states of wonder that cultivate awe and an ineffable appreciation of life.

8 While many proverbs affirm that the just will be rewarded and the unjust punished, this proverb makes it clear that it is God who will do the punishing. The ancient Hebrews were not yet in possession of a detailed doctrine of the afterlife and still believed that reward and punishment would come in this life. Just how that would come about, however, is up to God and may not be so obvious to human beings seeking justice as they define it.

30:15B–16

There are three things that are never satisfied,
truly four that never say *enough!*
The grave, a barren womb, parched land, and fire—these are
   never satisfied.

30:17

The eye that mocks its father and scorns its mother
is plucked out by ravens and consumed by young eagles.

30:18–19

There are three things beyond my comprehension,
a fourth thing, too, is beyond my ken:
the flight of an eagle in the sky;
the slithering of a serpent over a rock;
the course of a ship in the midst of the ocean;
and the passionate love of two young people.[7]

30:20

Those who gorge on evil and
wipe their lips saying, *I've done no wrong,*
their deeds are known to God.[8]

(continued on page 225)

9 The world of the ancients was one of clear hierarchies of power. Upsetting that hierarchy would render society unstable and topple what order there was. Here we are told of four instabilities that must be avoided:

- A slave who comes to rule suggests a level of class mobility that the ancients found threatening.
- A liar who profits from lying may refer to a person who sells false testimony in the courts, bringing the entire justice system into doubt.
- A prostitute who marries in order to trick her husband into supporting children she will have with other men can pervert the system of inheritance upon which families depend.
- A maid who seduces her master into divorcing his wife undermines the sanctity of marriage.

30:21–23
Three things disturb the natural order and
bring trembling to the earth,
a fourth she cannot bear:
a slave who becomes king;
a liar who profits from his lies;
a prostitute who marries;
a maid who marries her mistress's husband.[9]

30:24–28
There are four creatures whose instincts should guide us:
ants are a nation of little strength, yet they are always
     prepared for winter;
rabbits are not mighty, yet they make their home in the rocks;
locusts have no king, yet when they swarm they do so as one;
spiders may live in palaces, yet they are not too proud to
     catch their own food.

30:29–31
There are three who sleep securely,
a fourth who walks with confidence:
the lion is the strongest of creatures and is not afraid of
     anything;
the greyhound,
the he-goat, and
the king whose armies repel aggression.

(continued on page 227)

10 You cannot avoid feeling angry any more than you can avoid any other emotion to which we humans are prone. The way of the wise isn't to quell feelings or somehow avoid feeling them, but to avoid feeding them once they are felt.

30:32–33
If you have been hurt,
do not give in to anger,
and silence thoughts of revenge.
Just as churning milk produces butter,
and twisting a nose causes bleeding,
so nursing anger ends in violence.[10]

1 In the Hebrew the child's name is given: Lemuel, who is said to be "king of Massa." Again, this "name" is unique to Proverbs, and no such king is mentioned anywhere else in the Bible. In Hebrew, *lemuel* means "one who belongs to God." I suggest this is a section to be read as a mother's guide to raising a child in harmony with God and godliness.

2 Notice she doesn't oppose passion or power and only urges us not to fall victim to them.

3 Her concern is that we do nothing to cloud our vision, for when our thinking is muddy, we are easily persuaded to seek to add to our power by exploiting the poor and powerless.

4 Yet drinking in moderation, drinking without endangering our reason and our compassion, is not a problem and may even bring some joy to those who suffer.

5 This is what the wise mother wants her children to be: the prophetic voice of the poor.

☐ A Mother's Advice

31:1–2
The advice of a mother, a solemn warning to her child:[1]
I raised you and bore you and vowed all my love to you—
so listen, my child, to my advice:

31:3
Do not be carried away by passion
nor enslaved by power.[2]

31:4–7
Drunkenness and alcoholism are not appropriate for the godly.
Neither wine nor beer befits one who seeks the truth.
Strong drink clouds the mind and
leads to the corruption of justice for the poor.[3]
Yet a little beer may be a balm to the lost and those whose
    souls are bitter.[4]
Do not judge the suffering who drink for a moment's respite.

31:8–9
Open your mouth and speak for those who have no voice;
seek justice for those who have no champion.
Open your mouth and plead for the rights
of those who are poor and needy.[5]

(continued on page 231)

6 | While woven seamlessly into the earlier advice of the mother, this and the following verses of the Book of Proverbs is a separate section of its own marked by an alphabetical acrostic in Hebrew. If it were meant to stand alone and not merely stand out, this section would have been given its own chapter by the Masoretes, rabbis living during the seventh through eleventh centuries CE who produced the authoritative text of the Hebrew Bible. Since they chose to leave this acrostic as part of the mother's exhortation to her children, it is safe to say that this final section was thought to be part of her teaching. With this in mind, we can understand the final proverbs to be defining what kind of woman this mother wants her daughters to be and what kind of bride she wants her sons to marry.

7 | Throughout the Book of Proverbs the wise are admonished to honor both father and mother; here we learn why: wisdom is a woman's goal as well as a man's.

8 | This woman turns her home into a business. She buys wool and flax, which she uses not only to adorn herself and her household but also to sell to peddlers who market her wares to others (see below).

9 | It isn't only material goods that she seeks, but wisdom as well. She does not limit herself to the conventional knowledge of her people, but seeks the wisdom of the world's scholars wherever they may reside.

10 | Not only is she a craftswoman, but she is a landowner and a vintner as well, cultivating vineyards and selling her own wines.

11 | This woman is not about to submit to her husband, as Saint Paul hopes in his Letter to the Colossians 3:18, "Wives, be subject to your husbands as is fitting in the Lord," but celebrates her wisdom and her entrepreneurial spirit.

31:10–31

A woman of great accomplishment,[6]
who is worthy of her?
Her value is far beyond pearls.
She guides her husband's heart, and through her wisdom the
   household flourishes.[7]
She repays kindness with more kindness and is never driven
   to revenge.
She buys wool and flax, and works cheerfully in her home.[8]
She fills herself with wisdom from far-off lands, like a
   merchant ship laden with treasure.[9]
She rises early to attend to her household, her family, and
   her servants.
She plans her expenditure with care; she buys land and
   plants a vineyard.[10]
She is a tower of strength, her arms strong and secure.
She devotes herself to what is useful, and lets nothing snuff
   out her lamp.[11]
She reaches for the spinning wheel, and cradles the spindle
   in her palm.

(continued on page 233)

12 No matter how engaged she is with her family and her businesses, this woman is not ignorant of the plight of the poor and shares her wealth for the welfare of others.

13 No matter how strong her place in business, it is still the men who sit in legislative counsel. Yet it is her wisdom that guides the welfare of the city as she instructs her husband in the ways of wise governance.

14 In addition to her weaving and her vineyards, she also sells goods to peddlers, who sell her cloaks and belts in the marketplace.

15 This teaching seems out of place. Nowhere have we learned that this is a pious woman. Nowhere are we told that she prays to God or offers sacrifice in the Temple. On the contrary, she is a scholar of the world's wisdom and a businesswoman of much success. Where is God in this? The answer is found in the final verse.

16 Her life is her prayer; her integrity is her piety. Caring for her family and the poor is a sign of her godliness. Being productive and seeking out wisdom are signs of her devotion to God. The wisdom sages are not classical Pietists who abandon this world in search of another. They are deeply rooted in this world and equally devoted to making it just and right. This woman is a woman of God because her life is defined by creativity, ingenuity, and care for self and others. It is fitting that the Book of Proverbs ends with this lengthy definition of what a true sage is like. It is all the more compelling that the definition comes from a mother and speaks of women as the exemplars of the wisdom sage. While it is a fact of ancient life that patriarchy was the norm, it is heartening to see in the world of wisdom that the sages could reach beyond it.

She opens her hands to the poor, and her arms to embrace
the needy.[12]
She fears no winter, for she has clothed her household in
scarlet wool.
She makes for herself glorious bedspreads, and dresses of fine
linen and purple wool.
She counsels her husband, and her knowledge makes him
wise among the elders.[13]
She weaves cloth, and sells cloaks and belts to peddlers.[14]
She adorns herself with dignity, and is not afraid of the truth.
Her speech is full of wisdom, her tongue teaches human
kindness.
She anticipates the needs of her household, and does not eat
the bread of laziness.
Each morning her children feel blessed, her husband praises:
There are many wonderful women, but you surpass them all.
Do not be taken in by grace and beauty alone;
praise only the woman who devotes herself to God.[15]
The way she lives is evidence of her integrity;
her whole life is a testimony to her goodness.[16]

Afterword □

Solomon divides people into two categories: the wise and the ignorant. There is, most likely, much mingling of these in each of us, but for Solomon the distinction between them is clear and absolute:

> The wise learn from the softest whisper;
> the ignorant sleep through the loudest alarm. (10:5)

> Evil is the pastime of the foolish;
> wisdom the play of the wise. (10:23)

> The foolish justify their folly;
> the wise seek the counsel of the just. (12:15)

The Book of Proverbs speaks of people and life; it speaks to people who wish to live life well and find true satisfaction and tranquility. It is a how-to book, but unlike most such books, it is not given to easy recipes. Solomon does not prescribe exactly what we need to do, but rather shares with us timeless principles that we must put into practice in ways that are uniquely our own. We are all individuals. We cannot be reduced to a single prescription, but we can share a common set of principles. Our uniqueness is preserved in the way in which we apply the wisdom of Solomon, for no two of us will apply it in exactly the same way.

I hope that if you are reading the final pages of this book you have already read those that precede it. You have read and pondered, at least for a while, the challenge of Solomon's proverbs and guidance. I urge you not to put this book aside—read once and forgotten. Rather, now that you have some familiarity with the text, reread it with even greater concentration. Take one teaching at a time and ask yourself: How can I apply this principle in my life? How can I take upon myself the discipline of wisdom, the instruction of Lady Wisdom who calls to me from within Solomon's words?

Solomon has given voice to Wisdom. You must give her legs.

Bibliography □

Alter, Robert. *The Wisdom Books: Job, Proverbs, and Ecclesiastes*. New York: W.W. Norton & Company, 2010.

Barre, M., ed. *Wisdom, You Are My Sister*. Washington, DC: Catholic Biblical Association of America, 1997.

Bergant, Dianne. *What Are They Saying about Wisdom Literature?* New York: Paulist Press, 1984.

Bloom, Harold. *Where Shall Wisdom Be Found?* New York: Riverhead, 2004.

Boström, L. *The God of the Sages: The Portrayal of God in the Book of Proverbs*. Stockholm: Coronet Books, 1990.

Camp, C. V. *Wisdom and the Feminine in the Book of Proverbs*. Sheffield, UK: Almond Press, 1985.

Collins, J. J. *Jewish Wisdom in the Hellenistic Age*. Louisville: Westminster John Knox Press, 1997.

Crenshaw, James. *Old Testament Wisdom: An Introduction*. Atlanta: John Knox Press, 1971.

Dell, Katharine. *The Book of Proverbs in Social and Theological Context*. Cambridge: Cambridge University Press, 2009.

Fox, Michael. *Proverbs 1–9, A New Translation with Introduction and Commentary*. New York: Doubleday, 2000.

Hamam. *Commentary on the Book of Proverbs: Edition of the Armenian, English Translation, Notes and Introduction*. Leuven, Belgium: Peeters Publishers, 2005.

Hatton, Peter. *Contradiction in the Book of Proverbs: The Deep Waters of Counsel*. Hampshire, UK: Ashgate Publishing, 2008.

Howell, Toy. *A Critical and Exegetical Commentary on the Book of Proverbs*. Edinburgh: T&T Clark, 2009.

Lang, B. *Wisdom and the Book of Proverbs: An Israelite Goddess Redefined*. New York: Pilgrim, 1986.

Longman, Tremper, III. *How to Read Proverbs*. Downers Grove, IL: InterVarsity Press, 2002.

Perdue, Leo G. *Wisdom & Creation*. Nashville: Abingdon Press, 1994.

———. *Wisdom Literature: A Theological History*. Louisville: Westminster John Knox, 2007.

Perry, T. A. *God's Twilight Zone: Wisdom in the Hebrew Bible*. Peabody, MA: Hendrickson Publishers, 2008.

Rosenberg, A. J. *Proverbs: A New English Translation*. New York: Judaica Press, 1988.

Sandoval, Timothy J. *Money and the Way of Wisdom: Insights from the Book of Proverbs*. Woodstock, VT: SkyLight Paths, 2008.

Schroer, S. *Wisdom Has Built Her House: Studies on the Figure of Sophia in the Bible*. Translated by L. M. Mahoney and W. McDonough. Collegeville, MN: The Liturgical Press, 2000.

Scott, R. B. Y. *Proverbs, Ecclesiastes*. New York: Doubleday, 1965.

Shapiro, Rami. *The Divine Feminine in Biblical Wisdom Literature: Selections Annotated & Explained*. Woodstock, VT: SkyLight Paths, 2005.

———. *Ecclesiastes: Annotated & Explained*. Woodstock, VT: SkyLight Paths, 2010.

———. *Ethics of the Sages: Pirke Avot—Annotated & Explained*. Woodstock, VT: SkyLight Paths, 2006.

———. *Hasidic Tales: Annotated & Explained*. Woodstock, VT: SkyLight Paths, 2004.

———. *The Hebrew Prophets: Annotated & Explained*. Woodstock, VT: SkyLight Paths, 2004.

———. *Recovery—The Sacred Art: The Twelve Steps as Spiritual Practice*. Woodstock, VT: SkyLight Paths, 2009.

———. *The Sacred Art of Lovingkindness: Preparing to Practice*. Woodstock, VT: SkyLight Paths, 2006.

———. *Tanya, the Masterpiece of Hasidic Wisdom: Annotated & Explained*. Woodstock, VT: SkyLight Paths, 2010.

———. *The Way of Solomon*. San Francisco: HarperSanFrancisco, 2000.

———. *The Wisdom of Solomon*. New York: Bell Tower, 2002.

Surburg, Raymond F. *Introduction to the Intertestamental Period*. St. Louis: Concordia, 1975.

Swidler, Leonard. *Women in Judaism*. Metuchen, NJ: Rowman & Littlefield, 1976.

Von Rad, Gerhard. *Wisdom in Israel*. Nashville: Abingdon Press, 1972.

Waltke, Bruce. *The Book of Proverbs: Chapters 1–15*. Grand Rapids, MI: Eerdmans Publishing, 2004.

———. *The Book of Proverbs: Chapters 16–31*. Grand Rapids, MI: Eerdmans Publishing, 2005.

Westermann, Claus. *Roots of Wisdom*. Louisville: Westminster John Knox Press, 1995.

Whybray, R. N. *Wisdom in Proverbs*. Eugene, OR: Wipf and Stock Publishers, 1965.

Zuck, Roy. *Learning from the Sages: Selected Studies on the Book of Proverbs*. Eugene, OR: Wipf and Stock Publishers, 2003.

Notes ☐

Notes

Bible Study/Midrash

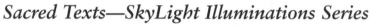

Sage Tales: Wisdom and Wonder from the Rabbis of the Talmud
By Rabbi Burton L.Visotzky Illustrates how the stories of the Rabbis who lived in the first generations following the destruction of the Jerusalem Temple illuminate modern life's most pressing issues. 6 x 9, 256 pp, HC, 978-1-58023-456-6 **$24.99**

The Modern Men's Torah Commentary: New Insights from Jewish Men on the 54 Weekly Torah Portions *Edited by Rabbi Jeffrey K. Salkin*
6 x 9, 368 pp, HC, 978-1-58023-395-8 **$24.99**

Righteous Gentiles in the Hebrew Bible: Ancient Role Models for Sacred Relationships
By Rabbi Jeffrey K. Salkin; Foreword by Rabbi Harold M. Schulweis;
Preface by Phyllis Tickle 6 x 9, 192 pp, Quality PB, 978-1-58023-364-4 **$18.99**

The Wisdom of Judaism: An Introduction to the Values of the Talmud
By Rabbi Dov Peretz Elkins 6 x 9, 192 pp, Quality PB, 978-1-58023-327-9 **$16.99**

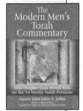

Sacred Texts—SkyLight Illuminations Series

Offers today's spiritual seeker an enjoyable entry into the great classic texts of the world's spiritual traditions. Each classic is presented in an accessible translation, with facing pages of guided commentary from experts, giving you the keys you need to understand the history, context and meaning of the text.

JUDAISM

The Divine Feminine in Biblical Wisdom Literature
Selections Annotated & Explained
Translation & Annotation by Rabbi Rami Shapiro; Foreword by Rev. Cynthia Bourgeault, PhD
5½ x 8½, 240 pp, Quality PB, 978-1-59473-109-9 **$16.99**

Ecclesiastes: Annotated & Explained
Translation & Annotation by Rabbi Rami Shapiro; Foreword by Rev. Barbara Cawthorne Crafton
5½ x 8½, 160 pp, Quality PB, 978-1-59473-287-4 **$16.99**

Ethics of the Sages: Pirke Avot—Annotated & Explained
Translation & Annotation by Rabbi Rami Shapiro
5½ x 8½, 192 pp, Quality PB, 978-1-59473-207-2 **$16.99**

Hasidic Tales: Annotated & Explained
Translation & Annotation by Rabbi Rami Shapiro; Foreword by Andrew Harvey
5½ x 8½, 240 pp, Quality PB, 978-1-893361-86-7 **$16.95**

The Hebrew Prophets: Selections Annotated & Explained
Translation & Annotation by Rabbi Rami Shapiro; Foreword by Rabbi Zalman M. Schachter-Shalomi
5½ x 8½, 224 pp, Quality PB, 978-1-59473-037-5 **$16.99**

Tanya, the Masterpiece of Hasidic Wisdom
Selections Annotated & Explained
Translation & Annotation by Rabbi Rami Shapiro; Foreword by Rabbi Zalman M. Schachter-Shalomi
5½ x 8½, 240 pp, Quality PB, 978-1-59473-275-1 **$16.99**

Zohar: Annotated & Explained
Translation & Annotation by Daniel C. Matt; Foreword by Andrew Harvey
5½ x 8½, 176 pp, Quality PB, 978-1-893361-51-5 **$15.99**

Or phone, mail or e-mail to: JEWISH LIGHTS Publishing
An imprint of Turner Publishing Company
4507 Charlotte Avenue • Suite 100 • Nashville, Tennessee 37209
Tel: (615) 255-2665 • www.jewishlights.com
Prices subject to change.

Children's Books by Sandy Eisenberg Sasso

Adam & Eve's First Sunset: God's New Day
Explores fear and hope, faith and gratitude in ways that will delight kids and adults—inspiring us to bless each of God's days and nights.
9 x 12, 32 pp, Full-color illus., HC, 978-1-58023-177-0 **$17.95** *For ages 4 & up*

Also Available as a Board Book: Adam and Eve's New Day
5 x 5, 24 pp, Full-color illus., Board Book, 978-1-59473-205-8 **$7.99** *For ages 0–4*
(A book from SkyLight Paths, Jewish Lights' sister imprint)

But God Remembered: Stories of Women from Creation to the Promised Land
Four different stories of women—Lilith, Serach, Bityah and the Daughters of Z—teach us important values through their faith and actions.
9 x 12, 32 pp, Full-color illus., Quality PB, 978-1-58023-372-9 **$8.99** *For ages 8 & up*

Cain & Abel: Finding the Fruits of Peace
Shows children that we have the power to deal with anger in positive ways. Provides questions for kids and adults to explore together.
9 x 12, 32 pp, Full-color illus., HC, 978-1-58023-123-7 **$16.95** *For ages 5 & up*

For Heaven's Sake
Heaven is often found where you least expect it.
9 x 12, 32 pp, Full-color illus., HC, 978-1-58023-054-4 **$16.95** *For ages 4 & up*

God in Between

If you wanted to find God, where would you look? This magical, mythical tale teaches that God can be found where we are: within all of us and the relationships between us. 9 x 12, 32 pp, Full-color illus., HC, 978-1-879045-86-6 **$16.95** *For ages 4 & up*

God Said Amen
An inspiring story about hearing the answers to our prayers.
9 x 12, 32 pp, Full-color illus., HC, 978-1-58023-080-3 **$16.95** *For ages 4 & up*

God's Paintbrush: Special 10th Anniversary Edition
Wonderfully interactive, invites children of all faiths and backgrounds to encounter God through moments in their own lives. Provides questions adult and child can explore together. 11 x 8½, 32 pp, Full-color illus., HC, 978-1-58023-195-4 **$17.95** *For ages 4 & up*

Also Available as a Board Book: I Am God's Paintbrush
5 x 5, 24 pp, Full-color illus., Board Book, 978-1-59473-265-2 **$7.99** *For ages 0–4*
(A book from SkyLight Paths, Jewish Lights' sister imprint)

Also Available: God's Paintbrush Teacher's Guide
8½ x 11, 32 pp, PB, 978-1-879045-57-6 **$8.95**

God's Paintbrush Celebration Kit
A Spiritual Activity Kit for Teachers and Students of All Faiths, All Backgrounds
9½ x 12, 40 Full-color Activity Sheets & Teacher Folder w/ complete instructions
HC, 978-1-58023-050-6 **$21.95**
8-Student Activity Sheet Pack (40 sheets/5 sessions), 978-1-58023-058-2 **$19.95**

In God's Name

Like an ancient myth in its poetic text and vibrant illustrations, this award-winning modern fable about the search for God's name celebrates the diversity and, at the same time, the unity of all people.
9 x 12, 32 pp, Full-color illus., HC, 978-1-879045-26-2 **$16.99** *For ages 4 & up*

Also Available as a Board Book: What Is God's Name?
5 x 5, 24 pp, Full-color illus., Board Book, 978-1-893361-10-2 **$7.99** *For ages 0–4*
(A book from SkyLight Paths, Jewish Lights' sister imprint)

Also Available in Spanish: El nombre de Dios
9 x 12, 32 pp, Full-color illus., HC, 978-1-893361-63-8 **$16.95** *For ages 4 & up*

Noah's Wife: The Story of Naamah

When God tells Noah to bring the animals of the world onto the ark, God also calls on Naamah, Noah's wife, to save each plant on Earth. Based on an ancient text.
9 x 12, 32 pp, Full-color illus., HC, 978-1-58023-134-3 **$16.95** *For ages 4 & up*

Also Available as a Board Book: Naamah, Noah's Wife
5 x 5, 24 pp, Full-color illus., Board Book, 978-1-893361-56-0 **$7.95** *For ages 0–4*
(A book from SkyLight Paths, Jewish Lights' sister imprint)

Bible Stories / Folktales

Abraham's Bind & Other Bible Tales of Trickery, Folly, Mercy and Love by Michael J. Caduto
New retellings of episodes in the lives of familiar biblical characters explore relevant life lessons.   6 x 9, 224 pp, HC, 978-1-59473-186-0 **$19.99**

Daughters of the Desert: Stories of Remarkable Women from Christian, Jewish and Muslim Traditions by Claire Rudolf Murphy,
Meghan Nuttall Sayres, Mary Cronk Farrell, Sarah Conover and Betsy Wharton
Breathes new life into the old tales of our female ancestors in faith. Uses tradition-al scriptural passages as starting points, then with vivid detail fills in historical con-text and place. Chapters reveal the voices of Sarah, Hagar, Huldah, Esther, Salome, Mary Magdalene, Lydia, Khadija, Fatima and many more. Historical fiction ideal for readers of all ages.
5½ x 8½, 192 pp, Quality PB, 978-1-59473-106-8 **$14.99**   Inc. reader's discussion guide
HC, 978-1-893361-72-0 **$19.95**

The Triumph of Eve & Other Subversive Bible Tales
by Matt Biers-Ariel
These engaging retellings of familiar Bible stories are witty, often hilarious and always profound. They invite you to grapple with questions and issues that are often hidden in the original texts.
5½ x 8½, 192 pp, Quality PB, 978-1-59473-176-1 **$14.99**
Also available: The Triumph of Eve Teacher's Guide
8½ x 11, 44 pp, PB, 978-1-59473-152-5 **$8.99**

Wisdom in the Telling
Finding Inspiration and Grace in Traditional Folktales and Myths Retold
by Lorraine Hartin-Gelardi
6 x 9, 192 pp, HC, 978-1-59473-185-3 **$19.99**

Religious Etiquette / Reference

How to Be a Perfect Stranger, 5th Edition: The Essential Religious Etiquette Handbook Edited by Stuart M. Matlins and Arthur J. Magida
The indispensable guidebook to help the well-meaning guest when visiting other people's religious ceremonies. A straightforward guide to the rituals and celebra-tions of the major religions and denominations in the United States and Canada from the perspective of an interested guest of any other faith, based on informa-tion obtained from authorities of each religion. Belongs in every living room, library and office. Covers:

African American Methodist Churches • Assemblies of God • Bahá'í Faith • Baptist • Buddhist • Christian Church (Disciples of Christ) • Christian Science (Church of Christ, Scientist) • Churches of Christ • Episcopalian and Anglican • Hindu • Islam • Jehovah's Witnesses • Jewish • Lutheran • Mennonite/Amish • Methodist • Mormon (Church of Jesus Christ of Latter-day Saints) • Native American/First Nations • Orthodox Churches • Pentecostal Church of God • Presbyterian • Quaker (Religious Society of Friends) • Reformed Church in America/Canada • Roman Catholic • Seventh-day Adventist • Sikh • Unitarian Universalist • United Church of Canada • United Church of Christ

"The things Miss Manners forgot to tell us about religion."
—Los Angeles Times

"Finally, for those inclined to undertake their own spiritual journeys ... tells visitors what to expect." *—New York Times*

6 x 9, 432 pp, Quality PB, 978-1-59473-294-2 **$19.99**

The Perfect Stranger's Guide to Funerals and Grieving Practices: A Guide
to Etiquette in Other People's Religious Ceremonies Edited by Stuart M. Matlins
6 x 9, 240 pp, Quality PB, 978-1-893361-20-1 **$16.95**

The Perfect Stranger's Guide to Wedding Ceremonies: A Guide to Etiquette
in Other People's Religious Ceremonies Edited by Stuart M. Matlins
6 x 9, 208 pp, Quality PB, 978-1-893361-19-5 **$16.95**

Spiritual Practice

Fly Fishing—The Sacred Art: Casting a Fly as a Spiritual Practice
by Rabbi Eric Eisenkramer and Rev. Michael Attas, MD
Illuminates what fly fishing can teach you about reflection, awe and wonder; the benefits of solitude; the blessing of community and the search for the Divine.
5½ x 8½, 192 pp (est), Quality PB, 978-1-59473-299-7 **$16.99**

***Lectio Divina*—The Sacred Art:** Transforming Words & Images into Heart-Centered Prayer *by Christine Valters Paintner, PhD*
Expands the practice of sacred reading beyond scriptural texts and makes it accessible in contemporary life. 5½ x 8½, 240 pp, Quality PB, 978-1-59473-300-0 **$16.99**

Haiku—The Sacred Art: A Spiritual Practice in Three Lines
by Margaret D. McGee 5½ x 8½, 192 pp, Quality PB, 978-1-59473-269-0 **$16.99**

Dance—The Sacred Art: The Joy of Movement as a Spiritual Practice
by Cynthia Winton-Henry 5½ x 8½, 224 pp, Quality PB, 978-1-59473-268-3 **$16.99**

Spiritual Adventures in the Snow: Skiing & Snowboarding as Renewal for Your Soul *by Dr. Marcia McFee and Rev. Karen Foster; Foreword by Paul Arthur*
5½ x 8½, 208 pp, Quality PB, 978-1-59473-270-6 **$16.99**

Divining the Body: Reclaim the Holiness of Your Physical Self *by Jan Phillips*
8 x 8, 256 pp, Quality PB, 978-1-59473-080-1 **$16.99**

Everyday Herbs in Spiritual Life: A Guide to Many Practices
by Michael J. Caduto; Foreword by Rosemary Gladstar
7 x 9, 208 pp, 20+ b/w illus., Quality PB, 978-1-59473-174-7 **$16.99**

Giving—The Sacred Art: Creating a Lifestyle of Generosity
by Lauren Tyler Wright 5½ x 8½, 208 pp, Quality PB, 978-1-59473-224-9 **$16.99**

Hospitality—The Sacred Art: Discovering the Hidden Spiritual Power of Invitation and Welcome *by Rev. Nanette Sawyer; Foreword by Rev. Dirk Ficca*
5½ x 8½, 208 pp, Quality PB, 978-1-59473-228-7 **$16.99**

Labyrinths from the Outside In: Walking to Spiritual Insight—A Beginner's Guide
by Donna Schaper and Carole Ann Camp
6 x 9, 208 pp, b/w illus. and photos, Quality PB, 978-1-893361-18-8 **$16.95**

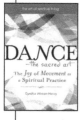

Practicing the Sacred Art of Listening: A Guide to Enrich Your Relationships and Kindle Your Spiritual Life *by Kay Lindahl* 8 x 8, 176 pp, Quality PB, 978-1-893361-85-0 **$16.95**

Recovery—The Sacred Art: The Twelve Steps as Spiritual Practice *by Rami Shapiro; Foreword by Joan Borysenko, PhD* 5½ x 8½, 240 pp, Quality PB, 978-1-59473-259-1 **$16.99**

Running—The Sacred Art: Preparing to Practice *by Dr. Warren A. Kay; Foreword by Kristin Armstrong* 5½ x 8½, 160 pp, Quality PB, 978-1-59473-227-0 **$16.99**

The Sacred Art of Chant: Preparing to Practice
by Ana Hernández 5½ x 8½, 192 pp, Quality PB, 978-1-59473-036-8 **$15.99**

The Sacred Art of Fasting: Preparing to Practice
by Thomas Ryan, CSP 5½ x 8½, 192 pp, Quality PB, 978-1-59473-078-8 **$15.99**

The Sacred Art of Forgiveness: Forgiving Ourselves and Others through God's Grace
by Marcia Ford 8 x 8, 176 pp, Quality PB, 978-1-59473-175-4 **$18.99**

The Sacred Art of Listening: Forty Reflections for Cultivating a Spiritual Practice
by Kay Lindahl; Illus. by Amy Schnapper 8 x 8, 160 pp, b/w illus., Quality PB, 978-1-893361-44-7 **$16.99**

The Sacred Art of Lovingkindness: Preparing to Practice
by Rabbi Rami Shapiro; Foreword by Marcia Ford 5½ x 8½, 176 pp, Quality PB, 978-1-59473-151-8 **$16.99**

Sacred Attention: A Spiritual Practice for Finding God in the Moment
by Margaret D. McGee 6 x 9, 144 pp, Quality PB, 978-1-59473-291-1 **$16.99**

Soul Fire: Accessing Your Creativity
by Thomas Ryan, CSP 6 x 9, 160 pp, Quality PB, 978-1-59473-243-0 **$16.99**

Thanking & Blessing—The Sacred Art: Spiritual Vitality through Gratefulness
by Jay Marshall, PhD; Foreword by Philip Gulley 5½ x 8½, 176 pp, Quality PB, 978-1-59473-231-7 **$16.99**

Inspiration

God of Me: Imagining God throughout Your Lifetime
By Rabbi David Lyon Helps you cut through preconceived ideas of God and dogmas that stifle your creativity when thinking about your personal relationship with God. 6 x 9, 176 pp, Quality PB, 978-1-58023-452-8 **$16.99**

The God Upgrade: Finding Your 21st-Century Spirituality in Judaism's 5,000-Year-Old Tradition *By Rabbi Jamie Korngold; Foreword by Rabbi Harold M. Schulweis* A provocative look at how our changing God concepts have shaped every aspect of Judaism. 6 x 9, 176 pp, Quality PB, 978-1-58023-443-6 **$15.99**

The Seven Questions You're Asked in Heaven: Reviewing and Renewing Your Life on Earth *By Dr. Ron Wolfson* An intriguing and entertaining resource for living a life that matters. 6 x 9, 176 pp, Quality PB, 978-1-58023-407-8 **$16.99**

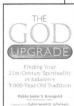

Happiness and the Human Spirit: The Spirituality of Becoming the Best You Can Be *By Rabbi Abraham J. Twerski, MD* Shows you that true happiness is attainable once you stop looking outside yourself for the source. 6 x 9, 176 pp, Quality PB, 978-1-58023-404-7 **$16.99**; HC, 978-1-58023-343-9 **$19.99**

A Formula for Proper Living: Practical Lessons from Life and Torah *By Rabbi Abraham J. Twerski, MD* 6 x 9, 144 pp, HC, 978-1-58023-402-3 **$19.99**

The Bridge to Forgiveness: Stories and Prayers for Finding God and Restoring Wholeness *By Rabbi Karyn D. Kedar* 6 x 9, 176 pp, Quality PB, 978-1-58023-451-1 **$16.99**

The Empty Chair: Finding Hope and Joy—Timeless Wisdom from a Hasidic Master, Rebbe Nachman of Breslov *Adapted by Moshe Mykoff and the Breslov Research Institute* 4 x 6, 128 pp, Deluxe PB w/ flaps, 978-1-879045-67-5 **$9.99**

The Gentle Weapon: Prayers for Everyday and Not-So-Everyday Moments— Timeless Wisdom from the Teachings of the Hasidic Master, Rebbe Nachman of Breslov *Adapted by Moshe Mykoff and S. C. Mizrahi, together with the Breslov Research Institute* 4 x 6, 144 pp, Deluxe PB w/ flaps, 978-1-58023-022-3 **$9.99**

God Whispers: Stories of the Soul, Lessons of the Heart *By Rabbi Karyn D. Kedar* 6 x 9, 176 pp, Quality PB, 978-1-58023-088-9 **$15.95**

God's To-Do List: 103 Ways to Be an Angel and Do God's Work on Earth *By Dr. Ron Wolfson* 6 x 9, 144 pp, Quality PB, 978-1-58023-301-9 **$16.99**

Jewish Stories from Heaven and Earth: Inspiring Tales to Nourish the Heart and Soul *Edited by Rabbi Dov Peretz Elkins* 6 x 9, 304 pp, Quality PB, 978-1-58023-363-7 **$16.99**

Life's Daily Blessings: Inspiring Reflections on Gratitude and Joy for Every Day, Based on Jewish Wisdom *By Rabbi Kerry M. Olitzky* 4½ x 6½, 368 pp, Quality PB, 978-1-58023-396-5 **$16.99**

Restful Reflections: Nighttime Inspiration to Calm the Soul, Based on Jewish Wisdom *By Rabbi Kerry M. Olitzky and Rabbi Lori Forman* 4½ x 6½, 448 pp, Quality PB, 978-1-58023-091-9 **$15.95**

Sacred Intentions: Morning Inspiration to Strengthen the Spirit, Based on Jewish Wisdom *By Rabbi Kerry M. Olitzky and Rabbi Lori Forman* 4½ x 6½, 448 pp, Quality PB, 978-1-58023-061-2 **$16.99**

Kabbalah/Mysticism

Jewish Mysticism and the Spiritual Life: Classical Texts, Contemporary Reflections *Edited by Dr. Lawrence Fine, Dr. Eitan Fishbane and Rabbi Or N. Rose* Inspirational and thought-provoking materials for contemplation, discussion and action. 6 x 9, 256 pp, HC, 978-1-58023-434-4 **$24.99**

Ehyeh: A Kabbalah for Tomorrow *By Rabbi Arthur Green, PhD* 6 x 9, 224 pp, Quality PB, 978-1-58023-213-5 **$18.99**

The Gift of Kabbalah: Discovering the Secrets of Heaven, Renewing Your Life on Earth *By Tamar Frankiel, PhD* 6 x 9, 256 pp, Quality PB, 978-1-58023-141-1 **$16.95**

Seek My Face: A Jewish Mystical Theology *By Rabbi Arthur Green, PhD* 6 x 9, 304 pp, Quality PB, 978-1-58023-130-5 **$19.95**

Zohar: Annotated & Explained *Translation & Annotation by Dr. Daniel C. Matt; Foreword by Andrew Harvey* 5½ x 8½, 176 pp, Quality PB, 978-1-893361-51-5 **$15.99** *(A book from SkyLight Paths, Jewish Lights' sister imprint)*

See also *The Way Into Jewish Mystical Tradition* in The Way Into… Series.

Meditation

Jewish Meditation Practices for Everyday Life
Awakening Your Heart, Connecting with God
By Rabbi Jeff Roth
Offers a fresh take on meditation that draws on life experience and living life with greater clarity as opposed to the traditional method of rigorous study.
6 x 9, 224 pp, Quality PB, 978-1-58023-397-2 **$18.99**

The Handbook of Jewish Meditation Practices
A Guide for Enriching the Sabbath and Other Days of Your Life
By Rabbi David A. Cooper Easy-to-learn meditation techniques.
6 x 9, 208 pp, Quality PB, 978-1-58023-102-2 **$16.95**

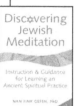

Discovering Jewish Meditation, 2nd Edition
Instruction & Guidance for Learning an Ancient Spiritual Practice
By Nan Fink Gefen, PhD 6 x 9, 208 pp, Quality PB, 978-1-58023-462-7 **$16.99**

Meditation from the Heart of Judaism
Today's Teachers Share Their Practices, Techniques, and Faith
Edited by Avram Davis 6 x 9, 256 pp, Quality PB, 978-1-58023-049-0 **$16.95**

Ritual/Sacred Practices

The Jewish Dream Book: The Key to Opening the Inner Meaning of Your Dreams *By Vanessa L. Ochs, PhD, with Elizabeth Ochs; Illus. by Kristina Swarner*
Instructions for how modern people can perform ancient Jewish dream practices and dream interpretations drawn from the Jewish wisdom tradition.
8 x 8, 128 pp, Full-color illus., Deluxe PB w/ flaps, 978-1-58023-132-9 **$16.95**

God in Your Body: Kabbalah, Mindfulness and Embodied Spiritual Practice
By Jay Michaelson
The first comprehensive treatment of the body in Jewish spiritual practice and an essential guide to the sacred.
6 x 9, 272 pp, Quality PB, 978-1-58023-304-0 **$18.99**

The Book of Jewish Sacred Practices: CLAL's Guide to Everyday & Holiday Rituals & Blessings *Edited by Rabbi Irwin Kula and Vanessa L. Ochs, PhD*
6 x 9, 368 pp, Quality PB, 978-1-58023-152-7 **$18.95**

Jewish Ritual: A Brief Introduction for Christians
By Rabbi Kerry M. Olitzky and Rabbi Daniel Judson
5½ x 8½, 144 pp, Quality PB, 978-1-58023-210-4 **$14.99**

The Rituals & Practices of a Jewish Life: A Handbook for Personal Spiritual Renewal *Edited by Rabbi Kerry M. Olitzky and Rabbi Daniel Judson*
6 x 9, 272 pp, Illus., Quality PB, 978-1-58023-169-5 **$18.95**

The Sacred Art of Lovingkindness: Preparing to Practice
By Rabbi Rami Shapiro 5½ x 8½, 176 pp, Quality PB, 978-1-59473-151-8 **$16.95**
(A book from SkyLight Paths, Jewish Lights' sister imprint)

Science Fiction/Mystery & Detective Fiction

Criminal Kabbalah: An Intriguing Anthology of Jewish Mystery & Detective Fiction *Edited by Lawrence W. Raphael; Foreword by Laurie R. King*
All-new stories from twelve of today's masters of mystery and detective fiction—sure to delight mystery buffs of all faith traditions.
6 x 9, 256 pp, Quality PB, 978-1-58023-109-1 **$16.95**

Mystery Midrash: An Anthology of Jewish Mystery & Detective Fiction
Edited by Lawrence W. Raphael; Preface by Joel Siegel
6 x 9, 304 pp, Quality PB, 978-1-58023-055-1 **$16.95**

Wandering Stars: An Anthology of Jewish Fantasy & Science Fiction
Edited by Jack Dann; Introduction by Isaac Asimov
6 x 9, 272 pp, Quality PB, 978-1-58023-005-6 **$18.99**

More Wandering Stars: An Anthology of Outstanding Stories of Jewish Fantasy and Science Fiction *Edited by Jack Dann; Introduction by Isaac Asimov*
6 x 9, 192 pp, Quality PB, 978-1-58023-063-6 **$16.95**

Spirituality

Repentance: The Meaning and Practice of *Teshuvah*
By Dr. Louis E. Newman; Foreword by Rabbi Harold M. Schulweis; Preface by Rabbi Karyn D. Kedar
Examines both the practical and philosophical dimensions of *teshuvah*, Judaism's core religious-moral teaching on repentance, and its value for us—Jews and non-Jews alike—today. 6 x 9, 256 pp, HC, 978-1-58023-426-9 **$24.99**

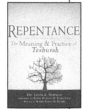

Tanya, the Masterpiece of Hasidic Wisdom
Selections Annotated & Explained
Translation & Annotation by Rabbi Rami Shapiro; Foreword by Rabbi Zalman M. Schachter-Shalomi
Brings the genius of *Tanya*, one of the most powerful books of Jewish wisdom, to anyone seeking to deepen their understanding of the soul.
5½ x 8½, 240 pp, Quality PB, 978-1-59473-275-1 **$16.99**
(A book from SkyLight Paths, Jewish Lights' sister imprint)

Aleph-Bet Yoga: Embodying the Hebrew Letters for Physical and Spiritual Well-Being
By Steven A. Rapp; Foreword by Tamar Frankiel, PhD, and Judy Greenfeld; Preface by Hart Lazer
7 x 10, 128 pp, b/w photos, Quality PB, Lay-flat binding, 978-1-58023-162-6 **$16.95**

A Book of Life: Embracing Judaism as a Spiritual Practice
By Rabbi Michael Strassfeld 6 x 9, 544 pp, Quality PB, 978-1-58023-247-0 **$19.99**

Bringing the Psalms to Life: How to Understand and Use the Book of Psalms
By Rabbi Daniel F. Polish, PhD 6 x 9, 208 pp, Quality PB, 978-1-58023-157-2 **$16.95**

Does the Soul Survive? A Jewish Journey to Belief in Afterlife, Past Lives &
Living with Purpose *By Rabbi Elie Kaplan Spitz; Foreword by Brian L. Weiss, MD*
6 x 9, 288 pp, Quality PB, 978-1-58023-165-7 **$16.99**

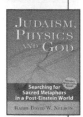

First Steps to a New Jewish Spirit: Reb Zalman's Guide to Recapturing the
Intimacy & Ecstasy in Your Relationship with God *By Rabbi Zalman M. Schachter-Shalomi*
with Donald Gropman 6 x 9, 144 pp, Quality PB, 978-1-58023-182-4 **$16.95**

Foundations of Sephardic Spirituality: The Inner Life of Jews of the Ottoman Empire
By Rabbi Marc D. Angel, PhD 6 x 9, 224 pp, Quality PB, 978-1-58023-341-5 **$18.99**

God & the Big Bang: Discovering Harmony between Science & Spirituality
By Dr. Daniel C. Matt 6 x 9, 216 pp, Quality PB, 978-1-879045-89-7 **$16.99**

God in Our Relationships: Spirituality between People from the Teachings of
Martin Buber *By Rabbi Dennis S. Ross* 5½ x 8½, 160 pp, Quality PB, 978-1-58023-147-3 **$16.95**

The Jewish Lights Spirituality Handbook: A Guide to Understanding,
Exploring & Living a Spiritual Life *Edited by Stuart M. Matlins*
What exactly is "Jewish" about spirituality? How do I make it a part of my life?
Fifty of today's foremost spiritual leaders share their ideas and experience with us.
6 x 9, 456 pp, Quality PB, 978-1-58023-093-3 **$19.99**

Judaism, Physics and God: Searching for Sacred Metaphors in a Post-Einstein World
By Rabbi David W. Nelson 6 x 9, 352 pp, Quality PB, inc. reader's discussion guide,
978-1-58023-306-4 **$18.99**; HC, 352 pp, 978-1-58023-252-4 **$24.99**

Meaning & Mitzvah: Daily Practices for Reclaiming Judaism through Prayer, God,
Torah, Hebrew, Mitzvot and Peoplehood *By Rabbi Goldie Milgram*
7 x 9, 336 pp, Quality PB, 978-1-58023-256-2 **$19.99**

Minding the Temple of the Soul: Balancing Body, Mind, and Spirit through Traditional
Jewish Prayer, Movement, and Meditation *By Tamar Frankiel, PhD, and Judy Greenfeld*
7 x 10, 184 pp, Illus., Quality PB, 978-1-879045-64-4 **$18.99**

One God Clapping: The Spiritual Path of a Zen Rabbi *By Rabbi Alan Lew with Sherril Jaffe*
5½ x 8½, 336 pp, Quality PB, 978-1-58023-115-2 **$16.95**

The Soul of the Story: Meetings with Remarkable People
By Rabbi David Zeller 6 x 9, 288 pp, HC, 978-1-58023-272-2 **$21.99**

There Is No Messiah … and You're It: The Stunning Transformation of Judaism's
Most Provocative Idea *By Rabbi Robert N. Levine, DD*
6 x 9, 192 pp, Quality PB, 978-1-58023-255-5 **$16.99**

These Are the Words: A Vocabulary of Jewish Spiritual Life
By Rabbi Arthur Green, PhD 6 x 9, 304 pp, Quality PB, 978-1-58023-107-7 **$18.95**

Spirituality/Prayer

Making Prayer Real: Leading Jewish Spiritual Voices on Why Prayer Is Difficult and What to Do about It *By Rabbi Mike Comins*
A new and different response to the challenges of Jewish prayer, with "best prayer practices" from Jewish spiritual leaders of all denominations.
6 x 9, 320 pp, Quality PB, 978-1-58023-417-7 **$18.99**

Witnesses to the One: The Spiritual History of the *Sh'ma*
By Rabbi Joseph B. Meszler; Foreword by Rabbi Elyse Goldstein
6 x 9, 176 pp, Quality PB, 978-1-58023-400-9 **$16.99**; HC, 978-1-58023-309-5 **$19.99**

My People's Prayer Book Series: Traditional Prayers, Modern Commentaries *Edited by Rabbi Lawrence A. Hoffman, PhD*
Provides diverse and exciting commentary to the traditional liturgy. Will help you find new wisdom in Jewish prayer, and bring liturgy into your life. Each book includes Hebrew text, modern translations and commentaries from all perspectives of the Jewish world.

Vol. 1—The *Sh'ma* and Its Blessings
7 x 10, 168 pp, HC, 978-1-879045-79-8 **$29.99**
Vol. 2—The *Amidah* 7 x 10, 240 pp, HC, 978-1-879045-80-4 **$24.95**
Vol. 3—*P'sukei D'zimrah* (Morning Psalms)
7 x 10, 240 pp, HC, 978-1-879045-81-1 **$29.99**
Vol. 4—*Seder K'riat Hatorah* (The Torah Service)
7 x 10, 264 pp, HC, 978-1-879045-82-8 **$29.99**
Vol. 5—*Birkhot Hashachar* (Morning Blessings)
7 x 10, 240 pp, HC, 978-1-879045-83-5 **$24.95**
Vol. 6—*Tachanun* and Concluding Prayers
7 x 10, 240 pp, HC, 978-1-879045-84-2 **$24.95**
Vol. 7—Shabbat at Home 7 x 10, 240 pp, HC, 978-1-879045-85-9 **$24.95**
Vol. 8—*Kabbalat Shabbat* (Welcoming Shabbat in the Synagogue)
7 x 10, 240 pp, HC, 978-1-58023-121-3 **$24.99**
Vol. 9—Welcoming the Night: *Minchah* and *Ma'ariv* (Afternoon and
Evening Prayer) 7 x 10, 272 pp, HC, 978-1-58023-262-3 **$24.99**
Vol. 10—Shabbat Morning: *Shacharit* and *Musaf* (Morning and
Additional Services) 7 x 10, 240 pp, HC, 978-1-58023-240-1 **$29.99**

Spirituality/Lawrence Kushner

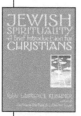

I'm God; You're Not: Observations on Organized Religion & Other Disguises of the Ego
6 x 9, 256 pp, HC, 978-1-58023-441-2 **$21.99**

The Book of Letters: A Mystical Hebrew Alphabet
Popular HC Edition, 6 x 9, 80 pp, 2-color text, 978-1-879045-00-2 **$24.95**
Collector's Limited Edition, 9 x 12, 80 pp, gold-foil-embossed pages, w/ limited-edition silkscreened print, 978-1-879045-04-0 **$349.00**

The Book of Miracles: A Young Person's Guide to Jewish Spiritual Awareness
6 x 9, 96 pp, 2-color illus., HC, 978-1-879045-78-1 **$16.95** *For ages 9–13*

The Book of Words: Talking Spiritual Life, Living Spiritual Talk
6 x 9, 160 pp, Quality PB, 978-1-58023-020-9 **$18.99**

Eyes Remade for Wonder: A Lawrence Kushner Reader *Introduction by Thomas Moore*
6 x 9, 240 pp, Quality PB, 978-1-58023-042-1 **$18.95**

God Was in This Place & I, i Did Not Know: Finding Self, Spirituality and Ultimate Meaning 6 x 9, 192 pp, Quality PB, 978-1-879045-33-0 **$16.95**

Honey from the Rock: An Introduction to Jewish Mysticism
6 x 9, 176 pp, Quality PB, 978-1-58023-073-5 **$16.95**

Invisible Lines of Connection: Sacred Stories of the Ordinary
5½ x 8½, 160 pp, Quality PB, 978-1-879045-98-9 **$15.95**

Jewish Spirituality: A Brief Introduction for Christians
5½ x 8½, 112 pp, Quality PB, 978-1-58023-150-3 **$12.95**

The River of Light: Jewish Mystical Awareness
6 x 9, 192 pp, Quality PB, 978-1-58023-096-4 **$16.95**

The Way Into Jewish Mystical Tradition
6 x 9, 224 pp, Quality PB, 978-1-58023-200-5 **$18.99**; HC, 978-1-58023-029-2 **$21.95**

Spirituality/Women's Interest

The Divine Feminine in Biblical Wisdom Literature: Selections Annotated & Explained *Translation & Annotation by Rabbi Rami Shapiro* 5½ x 8½, 240 pp, Quality PB, 978-1-59473-109-9 **$16.99** *(A book from SkyLight Paths, Jewish Lights' sister imprint)*

The Quotable Jewish Woman: Wisdom, Inspiration & Humor from the Mind & Heart *Edited by Elaine Bernstein Partnow* 6 x 9, 496 pp, Quality PB, 978-1-58023-236-4 **$19.99**

The Women's Haftarah Commentary: New Insights from Women Rabbis on the 54 Weekly Haftarah Portions, the 5 Megillot & Special Shabbatot *Edited by Rabbi Elyse Goldstein* 6 x 9, 560 pp, Quality PB, 978-1-58023-371-2 **$19.99**

The Women's Torah Commentary: New Insights from Women Rabbis on the 54 Weekly Torah Portions *Edited by Rabbi Elyse Goldstein* 6 x 9, 496 pp, Quality PB, 978-1-58023-370-5 **$19.99**; HC, 978-1-58023-076-6 **$34.95**

New Jewish Feminism: Probing the Past, Forging the Future *Edited by Rabbi Elyse Goldstein; Foreword by Anita Diamant* 6 x 9, 480 pp, Quality PB, 978-1-58023-448-1 **$19.99**; HC, 978-1-58023-359-0 **$24.99**

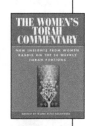

Spirituality/Crafts
(from SkyLight Paths, Jewish Lights' sister imprint)

Beading—The Creative Spirit: Finding Your Sacred Center through the Art of Beadwork *By Wendy Ellsworth*
Invites you on a spiritual pilgrimage into the kaleidoscope world of glass and color.
7 x 9, 240 pp, 8-page full-color insert, b/w photos and diagrams, Quality PB, 978-1-59473-267-6 **$18.99**

Contemplative Crochet: A Hands-On Guide for Interlocking Faith and Craft *By Cindy Crandall-Frazier; Foreword by Linda Skolnik*
Will take you on a path deeper into your crocheting and your spiritual awareness.
7 x 9, 208 pp, b/w photos, Quality PB, 978-1-59473-238-6 **$16.99**

The Knitting Way: A Guide to Spiritual Self-Discovery *By Linda Skolnik and Janice MacDaniels* Shows how to use knitting to strengthen your spiritual self. 7 x 9, 240 pp, b/w photos, Quality PB, 978-1-59473-079-5 **$16.99**

The Painting Path: Embodying Spiritual Discovery through Yoga, Brush and Color *By Linda Novick; Foreword by Richard Segalman*
Explores the divine connection you can experience through art.
7 x 9, 208 pp, 8-page full-color insert, b/w photos, Quality PB, 978-1-59473-226-3 **$18.99**

The Quilting Path: A Guide to Spiritual Self-Discovery through Fabric, Thread and Kabbalah *By Louise Silk* Explores how to cultivate personal growth through quilt making. 7 x 9, 192 pp, b/w photos, Quality PB, 978-1-59473-206-5 **$16.99**

The Scrapbooking Journey: A Hands-On Guide to Spiritual Discovery *By Cory Richardson-Lauve; Foreword by Stacy Julian*
Reveals how this craft can become a practice used to deepen and shape your life.
7 x 9, 176 pp, 8-page full-color insert, b/w photos, Quality PB, 978-1-59473-216-4 **$18.99**

Travel

Israel—A Spiritual Travel Guide, 2nd Edition: A Companion for the Modern Jewish Pilgrim *By Rabbi Lawrence A. Hoffman, PhD* 4¾ x 10, 256 pp, Illus., Quality PB, 978-1-58023-261-6 **$18.99**
Also Available: **The Israel Mission Leader's Guide** 5½ x 8½, 16 pp, PB, 978-1-58023-085-8 **$4.95**

Twelve Steps

100 Blessings Every Day: Daily Twelve Step Recovery Affirmations, Exercises for Personal Growth & Renewal Reflecting Seasons of the Jewish Year *By Rabbi Kerry M. Olitzky; Foreword by Rabbi Neil Gillman, PhD* 4½ x 6½, 432 pp, Quality PB, 978-1-879045-30-9 **$16.99**

Recovery from Codependence: A Jewish Twelve Steps Guide to Healing Your Soul *By Rabbi Kerry M. Olitzky* 6 x 9, 160 pp, Quality PB, 978-1-879045-32-3 **$13.95**

Twelve Jewish Steps to Recovery, 2nd Edition: A Personal Guide to Turning from Alcohol & Other Addictions—Drugs, Food, Gambling, Sex... *By Rabbi Kerry M. Olitzky and Stuart A. Copans, MD; Preface by Abraham J. Twerski, MD* 6 x 9, 160 pp, Quality PB, 978-1-58023-409-2 **$16.99**

Theology/Philosophy/The Way Into... Series

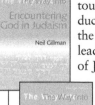

The Way Into... series offers an accessible and highly usable "guided tour" of the Jewish faith, people, history and beliefs—in total, an introduction to Judaism that will enable you to understand and interact with the sacred texts of the Jewish tradition. Each volume is written by a leading contemporary scholar and teacher, and explores one key aspect of Judaism. The Way Into... series enables all readers to achieve a real sense of Jewish cultural literacy through guided study.

The Way Into Encountering God in Judaism
By Rabbi Neil Gillman, PhD
For everyone who wants to understand how Jews have encountered God throughout history and today.
6 x 9, 240 pp, Quality PB, 978-1-58023-199-2 **$18.99**; HC, 978-1-58023-025-4 **$21.95**
Also Available: **The Jewish Approach to God:** A Brief Introduction for Christians
By Rabbi Neil Gillman, PhD
5½ x 8½, 192 pp, Quality PB, 978-1-58023-190-9 **$16.95**

The Way Into Jewish Mystical Tradition
By Rabbi Lawrence Kushner
Allows readers to interact directly with the sacred mystical texts of the Jewish tradition. An accessible introduction to the concepts of Jewish mysticism, their religious and spiritual significance, and how they relate to life today.
6 x 9, 224 pp, Quality PB, 978-1-58023-200-5 **$18.99**; HC, 978-1-58023-029-2 **$21.95**

The Way Into Jewish Prayer
By Rabbi Lawrence A. Hoffman, PhD
Opens the door to 3,000 years of Jewish prayer, making anyone feel at home in the Jewish way of communicating with God.
6 x 9, 208 pp, Quality PB, 978-1-58023-201-2 **$18.99**

The Way Into Jewish Prayer Teacher's Guide
By Rabbi Jennifer Ossakow Goldsmith
8½ x 11, 42 pp, PB, 978-1-58023-345-3 **$8.99**
Download a free copy at www.jewishlights.com.

The Way Into Judaism and the Environment
By Jeremy Benstein, PhD
Explores the ways in which Judaism contributes to contemporary social-environmental issues, the extent to which Judaism is part of the problem and how it can be part of the solution.
6 x 9, 288 pp, Quality PB, 978-1-58023-368-2 **$18.99**

The Way Into Tikkun Olam (Repairing the World)
By Rabbi Elliot N. Dorff, PhD
An accessible introduction to the Jewish concept of the individual's responsibility to care for others and repair the world.
6 x 9, 304 pp, Quality PB, 978-1-58023-328-6 **$18.99**

The Way Into Torah
By Rabbi Norman J. Cohen, PhD
Helps guide you in the exploration of the origins and development of Torah, explains why it should be studied and how to do it.
6 x 9, 176 pp, Quality PB, 978-1-58023-198-5 **$16.99**

The Way Into the Varieties of Jewishness
By Sylvia Barack Fishman, PhD
Explores the religious and historical understanding of what it has meant to be Jewish from ancient times to the present controversy over "Who is a Jew?"
6 x 9, 288 pp, Quality PB, 978-1-58023-367-5 **$18.99**; HC, 978-1-58023-030-8 **$24.99**

Theology/Philosophy

The God Who Hates Lies: Confronting & Rethinking Jewish Tradition
By Dr. David Hartman with Charlie Buckholtz
The world's leading Modern Orthodox Jewish theologian probes the deepest questions at the heart of what it means to be a human being and a Jew.
6 x 9, 208 pp, HC, 978-1-58023-455-9 **$24.99**

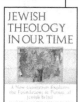

Jewish Theology in Our Time: A New Generation Explores the Foundations and Future of Jewish Belief *Edited by Rabbi Elliot J. Cosgrove, PhD; Foreword by Rabbi David J. Wolpe; Preface by Rabbi Carole B. Balin, PhD*
A powerful and challenging examination of what Jews can believe—by a new generation's most dynamic and innovative thinkers.
6 x 9, 240 pp, HC, 978-1-58023-413-9 **$24.99**

Maimonides, Spinoza and Us: Toward an Intellectually Vibrant Judaism
By Rabbi Marc D. Angel, PhD A challenging look at two great Jewish philosophers and what their thinking means to our understanding of God, truth, revelation and reason. 6 x 9, 224 pp, HC, 978-1-58023-411-5 **$24.99**

The Death of Death: Resurrection and Immortality in Jewish Thought
By Rabbi Neil Gillman, PhD 6 x 9, 336 pp, Quality PB, 978-1-58023-081-0 **$18.95**

Doing Jewish Theology: God, Torah & Israel in Modern Judaism *By Rabbi Neil Gillman, PhD*
6 x 9, 304 pp, Quality PB, 978-1-58023-439-9 **$18.99**

Hasidic Tales: Annotated & Explained *Translation & Annotation by Rabbi Rami Shapiro*
5½ x 8½, 240 pp, Quality PB, 978-1-893361-86-7 **$16.95***

A Heart of Many Rooms: Celebrating the Many Voices within Judaism
By Dr. David Hartman 6 x 9, 352 pp, Quality PB, 978-1-58023-156-5 **$19.95**

The Hebrew Prophets: Selections Annotated & Explained
Translation & Annotation by Rabbi Rami Shapiro; Foreword by Rabbi Zalman M. Schachter-Shalomi
5½ x 8½, 224 pp, Quality PB, 978-1-59473-037-5 **$16.99***

A Jewish Understanding of the New Testament *By Rabbi Samuel Sandmel;*
Preface by Rabbi David Sandmel 5½ x 8½, 368 pp, Quality PB, 978-1-59473-048-1 **$19.99***

Jews and Judaism in the 21st Century: Human Responsibility, the Presence of God and the Future of the Covenant *Edited by Rabbi Edward Feinstein; Foreword by Paula E. Hyman*
6 x 9, 192 pp, Quality PB, 978-1-58023-374-3 **$19.99**

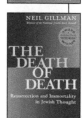

A Living Covenant: The Innovative Spirit in Traditional Judaism
By Dr. David Hartman 6 x 9, 368 pp, Quality PB, 978-1-58023-011-7 **$25.00**

Love and Terror in the God Encounter: The Theological Legacy of Rabbi Joseph B. Soloveitchik *By Dr. David Hartman* 6 x 9, 240 pp, Quality PB, 978-1-58023-176-3 **$19.95**

A Touch of the Sacred: A Theologian's Informal Guide to Jewish Belief
By Dr. Eugene B. Borowitz and Frances W. Schwartz
6 x 9, 256 pp, Quality PB, 978-1-58023-416-0 **$16.99**; HC, 978-1-58023-337-8 **$21.99**

Traces of God: Seeing God in Torah, History and Everyday Life *By Rabbi Neil Gillman, PhD*
6 x 9, 240 pp, Quality PB, 978-1-58023-369-9 **$16.99**

Your Word Is Fire: The Hasidic Masters on Contemplative Prayer
Edited and translated by Rabbi Arthur Green, PhD, and Barry W. Holtz
6 x 9, 160 pp, Quality PB, 978-1-879045-25-5 **$15.95**

I Am Jewish
Personal Reflections Inspired by the Last Words of Daniel Pearl
Almost 150 Jews—both famous and not—from all walks of life, from all around the world, write about many aspects of their Judaism.
Edited by Judea and Ruth Pearl 6 x 9, 304 pp, Deluxe PB w/ flaps, 978-1-58023-259-3 **$18.99**
Download a free copy of the *I Am Jewish Teacher's Guide* at www.jewishlights.com.

Hannah Senesh: Her Life and Diary, The First Complete Edition
By Hannah Senesh; Foreword by Marge Piercy; Preface by Eitan Senesh; Afterword by Roberta Grossman
6 x 9, 368 pp, b/w photos, Quality PB, 978-1-58023-342-2 **$19.99**

---

*A book from SkyLight Paths, Jewish Lights' sister imprint

Judaism / Christianity / Interfaith

Christians & Jews—Faith to Faith: Tragic History, Promising Present, Fragile Future *By Rabbi James Rudin*
A probing examination of Christian-Jewish relations that looks at the major issues facing both faith communities. 6 x 9, 288 pp, HC, 978-1-58023-432-0 **$24.99**

How to Do Good & Avoid Evil: A Global Ethic from the Sources of Judaism *By Hans Küng and Rabbi Walter Homolka* Explores how the principles of Judaism provide the ethical norms for all religions to work together toward a more peaceful humankind. 6 x 9, 224 pp, HC, 978-1-59473-255-3 **$19.99***

Getting to the Heart of Interfaith: The Eye-Opening, Hope-Filled Friendship of a Pastor, a Rabbi and a Sheikh
By Rabbi Ted Falcon, Pastor Don Mackenzie and Imam Jamal Rahman
Presents ways we can work together to transcend the differences that have divided us historically. 6 x 9, 192 pp, Quality PB, 978-1-59473-263-8 **$16.99***

Claiming Earth as Common Ground: The Ecological Crisis through the Lens of Faith *By Rabbi Andrea Cohen-Kiener* 6 x 9, 192 pp, Quality PB, 978-1-59473-261-4 **$16.99***

Modern Jews Engage the New Testament: Enhancing Jewish Well-Being in a Christian Environment *By Rabbi Michael J. Cook, PhD* 6 x 9, 416 pp, HC, 978-1-58023-313-2 **$29.99**

The Changing Christian World: A Brief Introduction for Jews
By Rabbi Leonard A. Schoolman 5½ x 8½, 176 pp, Quality PB, 978-1-58023-344-6 **$16.99**

Christians & Jews in Dialogue: Learning in the Presence of the Other
By Mary C. Boys and Sara S. Lee
6 x 9, 240 pp, Quality PB, 978-1-59473-254-6 **$18.99**; HC, 978-1-59473-144-0 **21.99***

Disaster Spiritual Care: Practical Clergy Responses to Community, Regional and National Tragedy *Edited by Rabbi Stephen B. Roberts, BCJC, and Rev. Willard W. C. Ashley Sr., DMin, DH*
6 x 9, 384 pp, HC, 978-1-59473-240-9 **$40.00***

Healing the Jewish-Christian Rift: Growing Beyond Our Wounded History
By Ron Miller and Laura Bernstein 6 x 9, 288 pp, Quality PB, 978-1-59473-139-6 **$18.99***

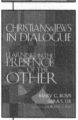

How to Be a Perfect Stranger, 5th Edition: The Essential Religious Etiquette Handbook *Edited by Stuart M. Matlins and Arthur J. Magida*
6 x 9, 432 pp, Quality PB, 978-1-59473-294-2 **$19.99***

InterActive Faith: The Essential Interreligious Community-Building Handbook
Edited by Rev. Bud Heckman with Rori Picker Neiss
6 x 9, 304 pp, Quality PB, 978-1-59473-273-7 **$16.99**; HC, 978-1-59473-237-9 **$29.99***

Introducing My Faith and My Community
The Jewish Outreach Institute Guide for the Christian in a Jewish Interfaith Relationship
By Rabbi Kerry M. Olitzky 6 x 9, 176 pp, Quality PB, 978-1-58023-192-3 **$16.99**

The Jewish Approach to Repairing the World (Tikkun Olam)
A Brief Introduction for Christians *By Rabbi Elliot N. Dorff, PhD, with Rev. Cory Willson*
5½ x 8½, 256 pp, Quality PB, 978-1-58023-349-1 **$16.99**

The Jewish Connection to Israel, the Promised Land: A Brief Introduction for Christians *By Rabbi Eugene Korn, PhD* 5½ x 8½, 192 pp, Quality PB, 978-1-58023-318-7 **$14.99**

Jewish Holidays: A Brief Introduction for Christians *By Rabbi Kerry M. Olitzky and Rabbi Daniel Judson* 5½ x 8½, 176 pp, Quality PB, 978-1-58023-302-6 **$16.99**

Jewish Ritual: A Brief Introduction for Christians *By Rabbi Kerry M. Olitzky and Rabbi Daniel Judson* 5½ x 8½, 144 pp, Quality PB, 978-1-58023-210-4 **$14.99**

A Jewish Understanding of the New Testament *By Rabbi Samuel Sandmel;*
Preface by Rabbi David Sandmel 5½ x 8½, 368 pp, Quality PB, 978-1-59473-048-1 **$19.99***

Righteous Gentiles in the Hebrew Bible: Ancient Role Models for Sacred Relationships *By Rabbi Jeffrey K. Salkin; Foreword by Rabbi Harold M. Schulweis; Preface by Phyllis Tickle* 6 x 9, 192 pp, Quality PB, 978-1-58023-364-4 **$18.99**

Talking about God: Exploring the Meaning of Religious Life with Kierkegaard, Buber, Tillich and Heschel *By Rabbi Daniel F. Polish, PhD* 6 x 9, 160 pp, Quality PB, 978-1-59473-272-0 **$16.99***

We Jews and Jesus: Exploring Theological Differences for Mutual Understanding
By Rabbi Samuel Sandmel; Preface by Rabbi David Sandmel
6 x 9, 192 pp, Quality PB, 978-1-59473-208-9 **$16.99**

*A book from SkyLight Paths, Jewish Lights' sister imprint

About Jewish Lights

People of all faiths and backgrounds yearn for books that attract, engage, educate, and spiritually inspire.

Our principal goal is to stimulate thought and help all people learn about who the Jewish People are, where they come from, and what the future can be made to hold. While people of our diverse Jewish heritage are the primary audience, our books speak to people in the Christian world as well and will broaden their understanding of Judaism and the roots of their own faith.

We bring to you authors who are at the forefront of spiritual thought and experience. While each has something different to say, they all say it in a voice that you can hear.

Our books are designed to welcome you and then to engage, stimulate, and inspire. We judge our success not only by whether or not our books are beautiful and commercially successful, but by whether or not they make a difference in your life.

For your information and convenience, at the back of this book we have provided a list of other Jewish Lights books you might find interesting and useful. They cover all the categories of your life:

Bar/Bat Mitzvah	Life Cycle
Bible Study / Midrash	Meditation
Children's Books	Men's Interest
Congregation Resources	Parenting
Current Events / History	Prayer / Ritual / Sacred Practice
Ecology / Environment	Social Justice
Fiction: Mystery, Science Fiction	Spirituality
Grief / Healing	Theology / Philosophy
Holidays / Holy Days	Travel
Inspiration	Twelve Steps
Kabbalah / Mysticism / Enneagram	Women's Interest

Stuart M. Matlins, Publisher

Or phone, mail or e-mail to: **JEWISH LIGHTS Publishing**
An imprint of Turner Publishing Company
4507 Charlotte Avenue • Suite 100 • Nashville, Tennessee 37209
Tel: (615) 255-2665 • www.jewishlights.com
Prices subject to change.

**For more information about each book,
visit our website at www.jewishlights.com**

About SKYLIGHT PATHS Publishing

SkyLight Paths Publishing is creating a place where people of different spiritual traditions come together for challenge and inspiration, a place where we can help each other understand the mystery that lies at the heart of our existence.

Through spirituality, our religious beliefs are increasingly becoming a part of our lives—rather than *apart* from our lives. While many of us may be more interested than ever in spiritual growth, we may be less firmly planted in traditional religion. Yet, we do want to deepen our relationship to the sacred, to learn from our own as well as from other faith traditions, and to practice in new ways.

SkyLight Paths sees both believers and seekers as a community that increasingly transcends traditional boundaries of religion and denomination—people wanting to learn from each other, *walking together, finding the way.*

For your information and convenience, at the back of this book we have provided a list of other SkyLight Paths books you might find interesting and useful. They cover the following subjects:

Or phone, mail or e-mail to: SKYLIGHT PATHS Publishing
An imprint of Turner Publishing Company
4507 Charlotte Avenue • Suite 100 • Nashville, Tennessee 37209
Tel: (615) 255-2665 • www.skylightpaths.com
Prices subject to change.

**For more information about each book,
visit our website at www.skylightpaths.com**

Printed in the USA
CPSIA information can be obtained
at www.ICGtesting.com
JSHW022213140824
68134JS00018B/1027